**continuing
education
series**

Leadership Essentials for Emergency Medical Services

AMERICAN ACADEMY OF ORTHOPAEDIC SURGEONS

John R. Brophy
EMS Supervisor & EMT-B Instructor
Liberty Health – Jersey City Medical Center
Jersey City, New Jersey

Captain
Edgewater Fire Department
Edgewater, New Jersey

JONES AND BARTLETT PUBLISHERS
Sudbury, Massachusetts
BOSTON   TORONTO   LONDON   SINGAPORE

AMERICAN ACADEMY OF ORTHOPAEDIC SURGEONS

World Headquarters
Jones and Bartlett Publishers
40 Tall Pine Drive
Sudbury, MA 01776
978-443-5000
info@jbpub.com
www.jbpub.com

Jones and Bartlett Publishers Canada
6339 Ormindale Way
Mississauga, Ontario L5V 1J2
Canada

Jones and Bartlett Publishers International
Barb House, Barb Mews
London W6 7PA
United Kingdom

American Academy of Orthopaedic Surgeons

Jones and Bartlett's books and products are available through most bookstores and online booksellers. To contact Jones and Bartlett Publishers directly, call 800-832-0034, fax 978-443-8000, or visit our website www.jbpub.com.

Substantial discounts on bulk quantities of Jones and Bartlett's publications are available to corporations, professional associations, and other qualified organizations. For details and specific discount information, contact the special sales department at Jones and Bartlett via the above contact information or send an email to specialsales@jbpub.com.

This textbook is intended solely as a guide to the appropriate procedures to be employed when rendering emergency care to the sick and injured. It is not intended as a statement of the standards of care required in any particular situation, because circumstances and the patient's physical condition can vary widely from one emergency to another. Nor is it intended that this textbook shall in any way advise emergency personnel concerning legal authority to perform the activities or procedures discussed. Such local determination should be made only with the aid of legal counsel.

Additional photographic and illustration credits appear on page 116, which constitutes a continuation of the copyright page.

Production Credits
Chief Executive Officer: Clayton Jones
Chief Operating Officer: Don W. Jones, Jr.
President, Higher Education and Professional Publishing: Robert W. Holland, Jr.
V.P., Sales: William J. Kane
V.P., Design and Production: Anne Spencer
V.P., Manufacturing and Inventory Control: Therese Connell
Publisher: Kimberly Brophy
Acquisitions Editor—EMS: Christine Emerton
Managing Editor: Carol Guerrero
Associate Editor: Karen Greene

Associate Production Editor: Sarah Bayle
Director of Marketing: Alisha Weisman
Associate Marketing Manager: Meagan Norlund
Composition: Shepherd, Inc.
Cover Design: Kristin E. Parker
Text Design: Shawn Girsberger
Photo Research Manager and Photographer: Kimberly Potvin
Cover Image: © Jones and Bartlett Publishers. Courtesy of MIEMSS.
Printing and Binding: Courier Corporation
Cover Printing: Courier Corporation

Library of Congress Cataloging-in-Publication Data
Brophy, John R.
  Leadership essentials for emergency medical services / John R. Brophy, American Academy of Orthopaedic Surgeons.
    p. ; cm.
  Includes index.
  ISBN-13: 978-0-7637-5875-2
  ISBN-10: 0-7637-5875-2
  1. Emergency medical services—management. 2. Leadership. I. American Academy of Orthopaedic Surgeons. II. Title.
  [DNLM: 1. Emergency Medical Services. 2. Leadership. WX 215 B869L 2009]
  RA645.5.B763 2009
  362.18—dc22
                              2008045000
6048
Printed in the United States of America
13 12 11 10 09   10 9 8 7 6 5 4 3 2 1

Dedication

This book is dedicated with love and affection to my Mom, Catherine G. Heldon, who provided me with her unwavering support and the encouragement to be the best I can be.

Contents

Resource Preview

This text is designed to provide EMTs and paramedics of every level with a clear examination of leadership as well as the tools to become a successful and effective leader in any situation. The following features have been specially constructed to illustrate leadership in many different contexts and to challenge the reader to think like a true leader:

Language of Leadership In attaining the status of a true leader, readers must be prepared with a set of vital vocabulary to apply to everyday situations. These clear definitions are easy to understand and can be directly translated into use in the real world.

Quotations of Leadership These quotations come from a wide variety of EMS and leadership experts and communicate the knowledge and experience of a variety of public figures.

Leadership Through the Hollywood Lens Taking a unique look at leadership in film and television, this feature applies popular culture in a fun, yet educational manner. Readers will easily recognize familiar characters and will quickly relate the lessons of these fictional scenarios to their own lives.

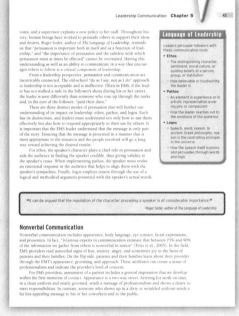

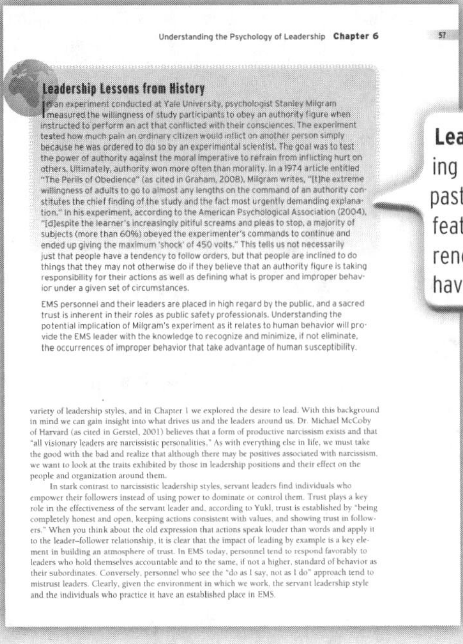
Understanding the Psychology of Leadership Chapter 6 57

Leadership Lessons from History

In an experiment conducted at Yale University, psychologist Stanley Milgram measured the willingness of study participants to obey an authority figure when instructed to perform an act that conflicted with their consciences. The experiment tested how much pain an ordinary citizen would inflict on another person simply because he was ordered to do so by an experimental scientist. The goal was to test the power of authority against the moral imperative to refrain from inflicting hurt on others. Ultimately, authority won more often than morality. In a 1974 article entitled "The Perils of Obedience" (as cited in Graham, 2008), Milgram writes, "[t]he extreme willingness of adults to go to almost any lengths on the command of an authority constitutes the chief finding of the study and the fact most urgently demanding explanation." In his experiment, according to the American Psychological Association (2004), "[d]espite the learner's increasingly pitiful screams and pleas to stop, a majority of subjects (more than 60%) obeyed the experimenter's commands to continue and ended up giving the maximum 'shock' of 450 volts." This tells us not necessarily just that people have a tendency to follow orders, but that people are inclined to do things that they may not otherwise do if they believe that an authority figure is taking responsibility for their actions as well as defining what is proper and improper behavior under a given set of circumstances.

EMS personnel and their leaders are placed in high regard by the public, and a sacred trust is inherent in their roles as public safety professionals. Understanding the potential implication of Milgram's experiment as it relates to human behavior will provide the EMS leader with the knowledge to recognize and minimize, if not eliminate, the occurrences of improper behavior that take advantage of human susceptibility.

variety of leadership styles, and in Chapter 1 we explored the desire to lead. With this background in mind we can gain insight into what drives us and the leaders around us. Dr. Michael McCoby of Harvard (as cited in Gerstel, 2001) believes that a form of productive narcissism exists and that "all visionary leaders are narcissistic personalities." As with everything else in life, we must take the good with the bad and realize that although there may be positives associated with narcissism, we want to look at the traits exhibited by those in leadership positions and their effect on the people and organization around them.

In stark contrast to narcissistic leadership styles, servant leaders find individuals who empower their followers instead of using power to dominate or control them. Trust plays a key role in the effectiveness of the servant leader and, according to Yukl, trust is established by "being completely honest and open, keeping actions consistent with values, and showing trust in followers." When you think about the old expression that actions speak louder than words and apply it to the leader–follower relationship, it is clear that the impact of leading by example is a key element in building an atmosphere of trust. In EMS today, personnel tend to respond favorably to leaders who hold themselves accountable and to the same, if not a higher, standard of behavior as their subordinates. Conversely, personnel who see the "do as I say, not as I do" approach tend to mistrust leaders. Clearly, given the environment in which we work, the servant leadership style and the individuals who practice it have an established place in EMS.

Leadership Lessons from History Learning from the successes and mistakes of the past is vital for every aspiring leader. This feature examines some of the nation's most renowned leaders, and reviews events that have irrevocably changed our nation.

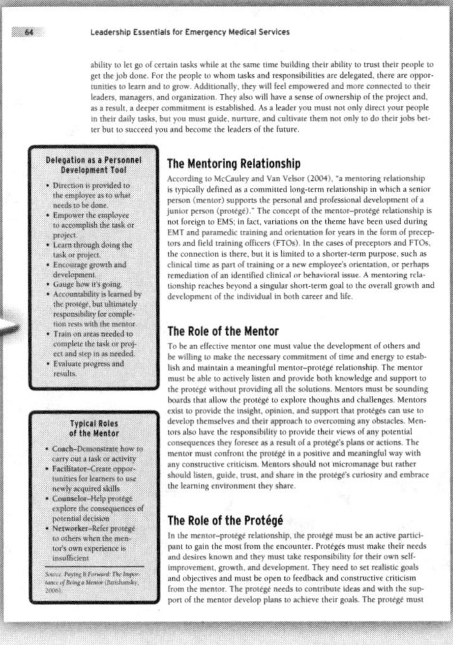
64 Leadership Essentials for Emergency Medical Services

ability to let go of certain tasks while at the same time building their ability to trust their people to get the job done. For the people to whom tasks and responsibilities are delegated, there are opportunities to learn and to grow. Additionally, they will feel empowered and more connected to their leaders, managers, and organization. They also will have a sense of ownership of the project and, as a result, a deeper commitment is established. As a leader you must not only direct your people in their daily tasks, but you must guide, nurture, and cultivate them not only to do their jobs better but to succeed you and become the leaders of the future.

Delegation as a Personnel Development Tool

- Direction is provided to the employee as to what needs to be done.
- Empower the employee to accomplish the task or project.
- Learn through doing the task or project.
- Encourage growth and development.
- Gauge how it's going.
- Accountability is learned by the protégé, but ultimately responsibility for completion rests with the mentor.
- Train on areas needed to complete the task or project and step in as needed.
- Evaluate progress and results.

Typical Roles of the Mentor

- Coach–Demonstrate how to carry out a task or activity
- Facilitator–Create opportunities for learners to use newly acquired skills
- Counselor–Help protégé explore the consequences of potential decision
- Networker–Refer protégé to others when the mentor's own experience is insufficient

Source: *Paying It Forward: The Importance of Being a Mentor* (Dzirkalis, 2006).

The Mentoring Relationship

According to McCauley and Van Velsor (2004), "a mentoring relationship is typically defined as a committed long-term relationship in which a senior person (mentor) supports the personal and professional development of a junior person (protégé)." The concept of the mentor–protégé relationship is not foreign to EMS; in fact, variations on the theme have been used during EMT and paramedic training and orientation for years in the form of preceptors and field training officers (FTOs). In the cases of preceptors and FTOs, the connection is there, but it is limited to a shorter-term purpose, such as clinical time as part of training or a new employee's orientation, or perhaps remediation of an identified clinical or behavioral issue. A mentoring relationship reaches beyond a singular short-term goal to the overall growth and development of the individual in both career and life.

The Role of the Mentor

To be an effective mentor one must value the development of others and be willing to make the necessary commitment of time and energy to establish and maintain a meaningful mentor–protégé relationship. The mentor must be able to actively listen and provide both knowledge and support to the protégé without providing all the solutions. Mentors must be sounding boards that allow the protégé to explore thoughts and challenges. Mentors exist to provide the insight, opinion, and support that protégés can use to develop themselves and their approach to overcoming any obstacles. Mentors also have the responsibility to provide their views of any potential consequences they foresee as a result of a protégé's plans or actions. The mentor must confront the protégé in a positive and meaningful way with any constructive criticism. Mentors should not micromanage but rather should listen, guide, trust, and share in the protégé's curiosity and embrace the learning environment they share.

The Role of the Protégé

In the mentor–protégé relationship, the protégé must be an active participant to gain the most from the encounter. Protégés must make their needs and desires known and they must take responsibility for their own self-improvement, growth, and development. They need to set realistic goals and objectives and must be open to feedback and constructive criticism from the mentor. The protégé needs to contribute ideas and with the support of the mentor develop plans to achieve their goals. The protégé must

Leadership Boxes This feature touches on a variety of issues that are pertinent to successful leadership, including stress warning signs, delegation, and the development of trust.

You Are the EMS Leader Test yourself: what kind of leader will you be in the real world? These situational examples call on readers to apply their newly acquired knowledge to dilemmas that they will face on the job. Pertinent questions place new leaders in the field, in the office, and in situations that may require positive reinforcement or disciplinary action.

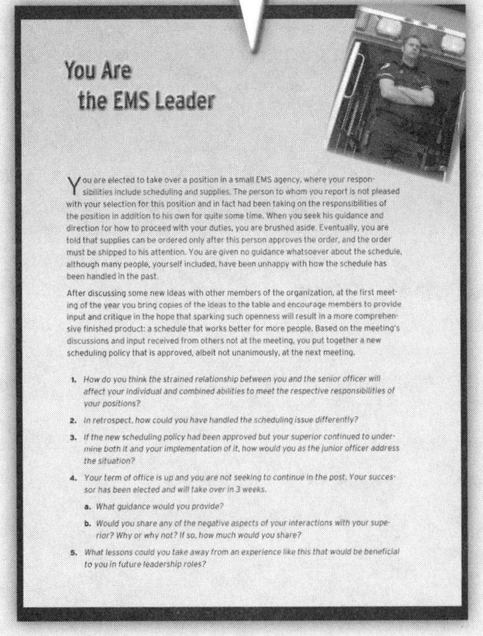
You Are the EMS Leader

You are elected to take over a position in a small EMS agency, where your responsibilities include scheduling and supplies. The person to whom you report is not pleased with your selection for this position and in fact had been taking on the responsibilities of the position in addition to his own for quite some time. When you seek his guidance and direction for how to proceed with your duties, you are brushed aside. Eventually, you are told that supplies can be ordered only after this person approves the order, and the order must be shipped to his attention. You are given no guidance whatsoever about the schedule, although many people, yourself included, have been unhappy with how the schedule has been handled in the past.

After discussing some new ideas with other members of the organization, at the first meeting of the year you bring copies of the ideas to the table and encourage members to provide input and critique in the hope that sparking such openness will result in a more comprehensive finished product: a schedule that works better for more people. Based on the meeting's discussions and input received from others not at the meeting, you put together a new scheduling policy that is approved, albeit not unanimously, at the next meeting.

1. *How do you think the strained relationship between you and the senior officer will affect your individual and combined abilities to meet the respective responsibilities of your positions?*
2. *In retrospect, how could you have handled the scheduling issue differently?*
3. *If the new scheduling policy had been approved but your superior continued to undermine both it and your implementation of it, how would you as the junior officer address the situation?*
4. *Your term of office is up and you are not seeking to continue in the post. Your successor has been elected and will take over in 3 weeks.*
   a. *What guidance would you provide?*
   b. *Would you share any of the negative aspects of your interactions with your superior? Why or why not? If so, how much would you share?*
5. *What lessons could you take away from an experience like this that would be beneficial to you in future leadership roles?*

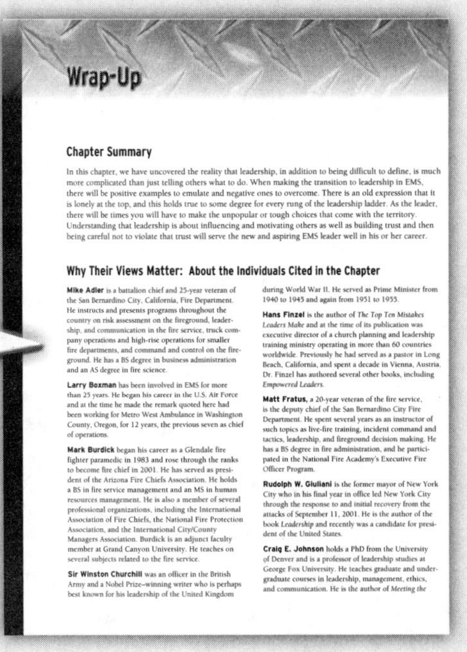
Wrap-Up

Chapter Summary

In this chapter, we have uncovered the reality that leadership, in addition to being difficult to define, is much more complicated than just telling others what to do. When making the transition to leadership in EMS, there will be positive examples to emulate and negative ones to overcome. There is an old expression that it is lonely at the top, and this holds true to some degree for every rung of the leadership ladder. As the leader, there will be times you will have to make the unpopular or tough choices that come with the territory. Understanding that leadership is about influencing and motivating others as well as building trust and then being careful not to violate that trust will serve the new and aspiring EMS leader well in his or her career.

Why Their Views Matter: About the Individuals Cited in the Chapter

Mike Adler is a battalion chief and 25-year veteran of the San Bernardino City, California, Fire Department. He instructs and presents programs throughout the country on risk assessment on the fireground, leadership, and communication in the fire service, truck company operations and high-rise operations for smaller fire departments, and command and control on the fireground. He has a BS degree in business administration and an AS degree in fire science.

Larry Boxman has been involved in EMS for more than 25 years. He began his career in the U.S. Air Force and at the time he made the remark quoted here had been working for Metro West Ambulance in Washington County, Oregon, for 12 years, the previous seven as chief of operations.

Mark Burdick began his career as a Glendale fire fighter paramedic in 1983 and rose through the ranks to become fire chief in 2001. He has served as president of the Arizona Fire Chiefs Association. He holds a BS in fire service management and an MS in human resources management. He is also a member of several professional organizations, including the International Association of Fire Chiefs, the National Fire Protection Association, and the International City/County Managers Association. Burdick is an adjunct faculty member at Grand Canyon University. He teaches on several subjects related to the fire service.

Sir Winston Churchill was an officer in the British Army and a Nobel Prize–winning writer who is perhaps best known for his leadership of the United Kingdom during World War II. He served as Prime Minister from 1940 to 1945 and again from 1951 to 1955.

Hans Finzel is the author of *The Top Ten Mistakes Leaders Make* and at the time of its publication was executive director of a church planning and leadership training ministry operating in more than 60 countries worldwide. Previously he had served as a pastor in Long Beach, California, and spent a decade in Vienna, Austria. Dr. Finzel has authored several other books, including *Empowered Leaders*.

Matt Fratus, a 20-year veteran of the fire service, is the deputy chief of the San Bernardino City Fire Department. He spent several years as an instructor of such topics as live-fire training, incident command and tactics, leadership, and fireground decision making. He has a BS degree in fire administration, and he participated in the National Fire Academy's Executive Fire Officer Program.

Rudolph W. Giuliani is the former mayor of New York City who in his final year in office led New York City through the response to and initial recovery from the attacks of September 11, 2001. He is the author of the book *Leadership* and recently was a candidate for president of the United States.

Craig E. Johnson holds a PhD from the University of Denver and is a professor of leadership studies at George Fox University. He teaches graduate and undergraduate courses in leadership, management, ethics, and communication. He is the author of *Meeting the*

Wrap-Up Concluding each chapter is the "Chapter Summary" and "Why Their Views Matter: About the Individuals Cited in the Chapter." Far beyond simply quoting experts in the field, the author introduces readers to new and familiar faces with brief biographies of the people who have inspired his own path to becoming a leader. These biographies complement the Quote Boxes found throughout the chapter.

Additional Resources

Instructor's ToolKit CD-ROM
ISBN: 978-0-7637-7286-4

- *PowerPoint® Presentations* correspond with the book and its features and can easily be personalized to suit each instructor's teaching style.
- *Lecture Outlines* provide a format for instruction and align with each of the PowerPoint® slides.
- *Teaching presentation tips and strategies* help instructors incorporate the unique features of the book into the classroom through engaging activities.

Acknowledgments

Jones and Bartlett Publishers would like to thank the following individuals for their review of the manuscript:

William L. Bingham, EFO, CFO
Fire Chief
City of Boynton Beach Fire Rescue Department
Boynton Beach, Florida

Mary F. Engler, RN, CCRN, EMT-B, and Fire Service Instructor
Captain
Coventry Volunteer Fire Association, Inc.
Coventry, Connecticut

Alan Heckman, BS, NREMT-P
Program Coordinator
George E. Moerkirk-Emergency Medicine Institute
Lehigh Valley Health Network
Allentown, Pennsylvania

Dolph Holmes, Firefighter/EMT
North Yarmouth Fire/Rescue
North Yarmouth, Maine
CPR & First Aid Instructor
Radio Communications Supervisor,
Maine Forest Service

Tom Lateulere
Chief, Education and Training
Suffolk County Division of Emergency Medical Services
Wading River, New York

John A. McCoy, BS, EMT-P
President
Emergency Incident Consultants
Spring Lake, North Carolina

Andrew H. Popick, BPA, NREMT-P
Battalion Chief
Davie Fire-Rescue
Coral Springs, Florida

David L. Sullivan PhD(c), NREMT-P
EMS/CME Program Director-Coordinator
Health Education Center
St. Petersburg College
Pinellas Park, Florida

Author Acknowledgments

As this book was in the reviewing and editing phase, I reflected upon just how many people both directly and indirectly contributed to it and my ability to see it through. Where to start a list of who to thank has, perhaps, as many possibilities as there are people to thank. Having contemplated who to thank and what to say, let me begin by thanking my primary proofreader, motivator, and very best friend Jill Clemens for keeping me on track. Her support and encouragement as well as critiques of my rough drafts played a huge part in making this whole project possible. I also need to thank Christine Emerton, Karen Greene, and everyone at Jones and Bartlett Publishers for not only providing me with the opportunity, but for guiding me through the process of writing my first book. Having been a reviewer for a number of books myself, I would be remiss if I didn't also specifically mention the time and feedback of the reviewers. Their contributions served to make this a better final product. To Professor Karen Kniep-Blanton and my Leadership Cohort classmates from Bellevue University, I say thanks for your support and constructive criticisms of my ideas as well as the opportunity to learn more about leadership and myself from all of you. Most importantly, thanks for the memories of the time we spent together. While on the topic of my college education, I must thank Liberty Health for their generous tuition reimbursement as well as Chris Rinn, Steve Cohen, and Joe Borer, who supported my promotion into ranks of the EMS management team. Without the chance they provided me, I would not have been able to afford to continue my education, apply what I had learned, or even write this book. I also need to thank my boss, Rick Sposa, as well as Captain Mark Rongone, USN, for being perhaps the two best "macro" managers I have ever worked for. It was through their encouragement, latitude, friendship, and trust in my abilities that I have been able to grow as a leader and a person. Over the course of my 10 years of Naval service there were countless others who had an impact upon me as a sailor, leader, and person. Among those who truly stand out are my Drill Instructor AMS1 (AW) Wayne

Sturgill, my best friend in Boot Camp Jason "Tugboat" Stanzione, my first LPO, now Senior Chief Hospital Corpsman Ed Christiansen, my first Chief, HMC Cathy Regan, and my former XO CDR Walter Klein. An extra special thanks is definitely in order for Captain Philip Landrigan, MC, USNR (RET), who not only greatly contributed to my growth and development when we served together in Africa, but who took the time, years later, to provide the foreword for this book. To perhaps my first mentor, Jim Lawlor, who left this world too soon as well as everyone at the firehouse, particularly Francis "Bubsy" Rock (may he also rest in peace), George Lasher, Dennis Sweeney, Bob Christiansen, Steve "Doc" Stewart, Sammy DeNorchia, and Deacon Bob Thomson: words cannot express the gratitude necessary for all that I have gained from their impact on my life. Finally, to my three life-long friends Dolph Holmes, Paul Ullrich, and John Bredin: I say thanks for putting up with me all these years. While John Bredin may still truly believe his now famous quip, "It's Brophy's world, we just live in it," I would especially like to thank him for all the late night "holy hour" discussions and his encouragement of my writing. It definitely played a large part in my successful completion of this book. To him, his students, and everyone specifically listed as well as those not listed who played a part in this book and in my life: I wish you all the very best that life has to offer.

Author Biography

John R. Brophy is an EMS Supervisor and EMT-B Instructor who has served as a fire department captain and U.S. Navy Corpsman. His EMS, fire, and military experience spans three decades and includes leadership positions at home and abroad. In addition to his experience as a provider and leader in the field, he has written a number of feature articles for a variety of national trade magazines and served on the review panels of a number of EMS textbooks.

Foreword

Leadership—the ability to bring people together, to help them to rise above themselves to accomplish great and heroic deeds that they could never accomplish alone—is essential in all collective human endeavors. Leadership is critical in business, medicine, government, and the military. These enterprises succeed and even succeed brilliantly when their leaders are strong, knowledgeable, focused, ethical, and compassionate. They fail when their leaders lack these qualities.

Nowhere is leadership more important than among emergency responders. Emergency responders are called in their work to address incredibly complex, dangerous, and often unprecedented situations for which there exist no "textbook" solutions. They face fire, floods, tornadoes, explosions, riots, shootings, and earthquakes. And in today's world, as the terrible events of September 11, 2001 so clearly taught us, emergency responders must be prepared to face the evil manifestations of terrorism—bombs and explosions as well as chemical, biological, and nuclear threats. These events typically unfold at lighting speed. Casualties mount. Confusion reigns. Communications may fail. Leadership is essential.

The central message of this very important book by John R. Brophy is one of optimism— namely, that leadership can be taught and that it can be learned. In this volume, which is targeted specifically to emergency medical responders, but that should be required reading for emergency responders of every category, John presents a logical, understandable, step-by-step guide to the teaching and learning of leadership. He stresses the fundamentals. He emphasizes the critical importance of ethics. He presents a feasible approach to mastering such essential basics of leadership as leading change, team building, and communications. His approach is based on decades of experience and the teaching of leadership that was pioneered in the military, refined in business, and then validated in careful academic studies. This is powerful information.

John R. Brophy is eminently well qualified to write this book. He has served for many years in the United States Naval Reserve as a Corpsman, including overseas duty in Thailand, Lithuania, Greece, Honduras, and in West Africa, where he and I served together. He is an EMS Supervisor and Fire Department Captain in New Jersey and was recognized by the President of the United States for his leadership in New Orleans during and following Hurricane Katrina. He lives what he preaches.

I highly recommend this book.

Philip J. Landrigan, MD, MSc
Professor and Chairman
Department of Community and Preventive
  Medicine
Mount Sinai School of Medicine
New York, New York

CAPT, MC, USNR (RET)
Deputy Command Surgeon General
New York Naval Militia

Chapter 1

Overview of Leadership Essentials

❙❙Leadership and learning are indispensable to each other.❚❚

—John F. Kennedy

Introduction

Leadership is a part of everyday life in emergency medical services (EMS) around the world. Understanding what leadership is and how it can affect patient care, personnel, and the EMS organization are of paramount importance to every individual who holds or seeks a position of leadership in the EMS community. In EMS, it is important to realize that leadership is more than simply having a title; it is having a passion and a desire to make a difference as well as having the courage to accept future challenges. Having this understanding is an important part of leadership development. It provides a deeper appreciation for both the positive and the negative impacts that result from the actions and mindset of EMS leaders.

In EMS, whether career or volunteer, the most likely path to an official leadership position begins as a provider of emergency care. One develops assessment and patient care skills over time. Simultaneously, one's confidence will gradually develop as well. This confidence will be mirrored in others' expectations, and trust will naturally build. Leadership and advancement opportunities will undoubtedly arise. Whether one receives an appointed promotion in career EMS or an elected promotion in volunteer EMS, proven skills, trust, and likeability are the keys to an individual's advancement. Once one is in a new position of greater responsibility, a whole new set of challenges will present additional leadership opportunities. New EMS leaders are often expected to somehow figure it out for themselves and are judged by subordinates, peers, and superiors based on how they address their new responsibilities. As a leader, you will find that sometimes, no matter what you do, there will as often be as many individuals who find fault with your actions

❚❚*Successful EMS systems employ people who recognize that leadership is not just about position or titles, but is a choice that one consciously makes.*❚❚

–Larry Boxman, Chief of Operations, Metro West Ambulance, &
Jason Rogers, Director of Training, Metro West Ambulance

> **"When you lead, everything you say and do is amplified in the organization's eyes."**
>
> –Battalion Chief Mike Adler, San Bernardino City Fire Department, & Deputy Chief Matt Fratus, San Bernardino City Fire Department

as who praise them. Leaders, particularly those in the public eye, will find themselves effectively "on stage" at all times. Their words and deeds will be subject to review by a variety of people having a variety of biases and agendas. Therefore, to increase the effectiveness of present and future EMS leaders, resources, education, and transitional insights into their new roles must be provided.

To better understand leadership and its role in and effects on EMS, we must first define leadership. While on the surface this may seem like a simple task, according to Stogdill (as cited in Yukl, 2006) "there are almost as many definitions of leadership as there are persons who have attempted to define the concept." In fact, "decades of academic analysis have given us more than 350 definitions of leadership" (Finzel, 2000). With that said, let's look at a few definitions of leadership and perhaps develop the beginnings of a definition specifically designed for EMS.

The Random House Webster's College Dictionary (Costello, 1992) defines leadership as "the position or function of a leader," "ability to lead," "an act or instance of leading; guidance; direction," or "the leaders of a group." Other definitions of leadership are

- "Leadership is the exercise of influence in a group context" (Bass, 1990, as cited in Johnson, 2005).
- "Leaders unify groups of people through mutually held values and goals and help them to achieve common objectives" (Salka, 2004).

If we reflect on our initial training, the development of our knowledge, the evolution of our skills, the building of our confidence, lessons learned in the field, and lessons learned through continuing education, it is clear that all EMS providers have quite a bit in common. As we progress through our careers, we have the opportunity to experience, remember, and reflect on the leadership we have provided or followed. In so doing, we form opinions about the positives and negatives of these experiences. "Leadership does not simply happen. It can be taught, learned, developed" (Giuliani & Kurson, 2002). As leaders in EMS emerge, their leadership style will build on the foundation laid for them in training and through early experiences in their careers with preceptors, supervisors, and officers. Those who aspire to positions of leadership often do so with a vision of who they want to emulate or what they want to change in their organization. This vision is frequently based on the insights aspiring leaders have gained through their experiences.

> **"If leaders don't know who they are, insecurity and the need to stay on top will cause them to make unwise decisions."**
>
> –John W. Stanko

The Desire to Lead

Although it is true that leadership skills and techniques can be taught (in fact, the purpose of this book is to serve as the centerpiece of a program for new and aspiring leaders in EMS), it is important to explore the reasons and motivations behind the desire to lead. To do so, let's first look at the leader as an individual. This is important in part because "if leaders don't know who they are, insecurity and the need to stay on top will cause them to make unwise decisions" (Stanko, 2000). Leaders have a vision of who they are and what they want to accomplish. However, there are often numerous motives behind one's desire to lead. For example, some seek power as an end in itself, whereas others seek power as a means to achieve their goals or visions. Leaders should ask themselves, What do I seek to accomplish in a particular role or position? I recall attending a class with a cross section of EMS leaders, both career and volunteer, from around the country. When one leader was asked, "Why have you been in the top position of leadership in your volunteer agency for such a long period of time?" the leader replied that no other member of the organization was capable of doing the job. To me, this reflected that this leader had no vision beyond maintaining the status quo. I also recall thinking how unfortunate it was that others in this leader's organization were not offered opportunities to lead and to grow that would also benefit their organization. It is important to note, however, that at no time did I question the original leader's dedication or her belief that her actions were in the organization's best interests. I realized from this experience the importance of providing leadership education to EMS leaders. This instance also reminded me that it is important for leaders to take frequent stock of themselves and their effectiveness. This will ensure that, at a minimum, each leader meets the responsibilities of his or her current position, maintains the original vision for filling that role, and is clear about his or her future vision for personal goals and the organization.

Making the Transition

To become an effective leader once in an official leadership position, one must realize that a title does not make a leader. What the title does do, however, is officially grant increased responsibility and the legitimate or "legal" authority to carry out new responsibilities. Making the transition from one of the crew to the one responsible for the crew will take time and presents its own unique set of challenges for the new leader and the followers alike. Mark Burdick, a fire chief from Arizona who began his career around the same time as I did back in the early 1980s, believes that when an individual is promoted, "it is more than just pinning the badge on and letting them learn by trial and error." I could not agree more. I can't help but wonder if Mark and other professionals across the country made some of the very mistakes that I did as I learned and grew as an officer in EMS and the fire service. Many of my colleagues must agree with what I learned from the mistakes of my career: that they are a great learning tool. Even the best trained and best educated among us are going to make mistakes. However, when transitioning from a staff position to a supervisory one, it is important to understand that the ownership of not only your mistakes but also the mistakes of your people will land squarely on your shoulders after you are promoted. With this in mind, as we move forward with our discussion of making the transition, it is important for new and aspiring leaders to understand the concepts of responsibility, authority, and accountability.

Responsibility

The first idea that new leaders must understand is responsibility and that, in their new role, they are now answerable for not just their own actions but also the actions of others. As a leader, one must realize that one is both responsible *for* and *to* one's subordinates. A leader must also understand that he or she now has a greater responsibility to the organization and must endeavor to uphold its values and enforce its policies. This includes maintaining and developing strong relationships with people who were once peers but are now subordinates. Leaders also have more responsibility for their personal behavior. New leaders must set the example and not allow or participate in inappropriate behavior. As leaders, we set an example with everything we do, and we must ask ourselves if the example we are setting is the one we want others to follow. For example, if we often show up late, we send the message that tardiness is okay. A fellow

"*Acting illegally or immorally not only subverts the organization's value system, it compromises authority.*"

–Stephen E. Kohn & Vincent D. O'Connell, authors of *6 Habits of Highly Effective Bosses*

Language of Leadership

- **Management**—The act or art of conducting, handling, controlling, or directing something through the judicious use of means to accomplish an end
- **Supervision**—The action or process of watching, directing, or guiding workers or the work done by others

EMS leader once shared his belief with me that if you hold a supervisory or management position, you are always in that role, even after hours. Although some may argue the legality or legitimacy of this opinion, the perception remains. In someone's eyes, for good or bad, anyone who holds an official leadership position will always be seen as a "boss." This concept of personal responsibility, both on and off duty, is a big part of leadership that is often overlooked or downplayed, but it is one that, if handled properly, will build trust and credibility with superiors, peers, and subordinates. In contrast, one lapse of judgment in this area can cause significant damage to the organization and set a leader back in personal and professional growth.

> **"**Leaders must weigh a host of loyalties or duties when making choices" and "noteworthy leaders put the needs of the larger community above selfish interests.**"**
>
> –Craig E. Johnson, Professor of Leadership Studies, George Fox University

Leadership Through the Hollywood Lens

In an episode of the television series "JAG," Navy JAG lawyer Lieutenant Commander Harmon Rabb, Jr (David James Elliott), is called on to investigate a naval aviation accident in the Nevada desert that resulted in the deaths of two civilians. As the investigation unfolds, Rabb discovers that the accident may have happened because Captain Gary Hochausen (Gary Graham), Rabb's former flying instructor, mentor, and long-time friend, cheated on his eye exams to maintain flight status. When Rabb is certain of his beliefs, he offers to help Hochausen resign, allowing Hochausen to avoid public embarrassment in return for his cooperation. This offer is flatly refused, leaving Rabb to choose between loyalty and responsibility. From a leadership perspective, however, one must wonder if, given their long-time relationship, Rabb perhaps should not have been investigating the incident in the first place. Additionally, this brings up the question of whether his offer would have been made by a more impartial investigator. In the end, Rabb is true to the responsibilities of his position. This comes at the personal cost of changing, if not ending, his friendship with Captain Hochausen in the process.

Making the transition to an official position of leadership involves increased responsibility and inevitably will create situations in which an EMS leader must balance his or her old beliefs, loyalties, and even friendships against the requirements of the new position. Unlike in the Navy and other very large organizations, the vast majority of EMS supervisors will not have the luxury of passing off an investigation of a former peer or partner because of the size of most EMS organizations. In short, how situations are handled will have short- and long-term effects as well as personal and professional repercussions on the leader, on the other people involved, and on the organization as a whole.

> **"If you are going to ask people to respect your authority, you'll need to lead by example."**
>
> –Vince Lombardi, Jr., author of *The Lombardi Rules*

Authority

In addition to the added personal and professional responsibility of a leadership position, there is the authority to perform the functions of the job. Clearly, by virtue of the title bestowed and the job description, the "legal" authority to perform tasks and make decisions does exist. However, authority goes far beyond the legal or legitimate authority to perform the duties and make the decisions incumbent on someone in an official position. Of equal and often even greater importance are earned authority and moral authority. Earned authority is about respect and trust, whereas moral authority hinges on honesty and integrity. Cultivating an atmosphere that promotes respect and trust will go a long way toward increasing the effectiveness of a leader while simultaneously improving the organization as a whole. This aspect of authority will take time and initially will be greatly affected by the manner in which the new leader conducted himself or herself both before and immediately following the promotion. Lorin Woolfe, who organized and delivered leadership development programs for such companies as E. F. Hutton and Manufacturers Hanover Trust, tells us that "honesty and integrity pay off long-term, though they may involve losses and sacrifices short term" (Woolfe, 2002). People in official leadership positions will often have to make unpopular decisions, and judgment will be passed from all angles. Subordinates will see a situation one way and peers and superiors will likely see it another. From a moral perspective, the most important aspect of the decision-making process is ensuring that the appropriateness of the situation is considered. It is with this consideration that integrity will be upheld, despite the potential plunge in popularity. Then, with time and distance, the memories of an unpopular but appropriate choice will fade away while a decision based on favoritism, a vendetta, or some other less-than-honorable consideration will likely be remembered with less favorable tribute. In short, authority goes well beyond a title and is greatly affected by the actions of the individual holding the position.

Delegation of Authority

As a leader, you will often find situations in which delegating a project to a subordinate or group of subordinates is an effective way to accomplish the task while at the same time developing their skills, your trust in them, and theirs in you. The catch is that although you, as the leader, may have delegated a project, the responsibility for its completion rests on your shoulders. Unlike in the past when you went to a superior who took responsibility for addressing a situation you brought to his or her attention, you are now the one responsible and the one who will be held accountable. Therefore, be certain not only to delegate the task or project but also to delegate the necessary authority to get it done. Provide deadlines that are achievable, guidance on how to proceed, and suggestions for what to do should subordinates stumble or otherwise require your assistance. When the task is completed, be sure to provide feedback and recognition for their efforts. Remember: You can delegate the task and the authority but not the responsibility.

Language of Leadership

- **Legal Authority**—The official authority that is inherent in the position or office that the leader holds
- **Moral Authority**—The authority derived from the leader's sense of responsibility to do what is proper and to step forward and take the lead even when not required
- **Earned Authority**—The authority that grows out of the respect, credibility, and leadership qualities that encourage others to follow

Leadership Lessons from History

On December 3, 1999, the Worcester Massachusetts Fire Department lost six fire fighters while searching for possible victims reported to be in the building. A MAYDAY was sounded and crews began searching for the fire fighters in distress. Some of the fire fighters who lost their lives that day did so while searching for the others. When District Chief Mike McNamee was advised that not just two, but at least four fire fighters were missing as a result of the rescue effort, he made what must have been the most difficult and heart-wrenching decision of not only his professional career, but also of his life. He weighed the risk versus the benefit of continuing the search, saw that conditions had significantly worsened, and made the decision to remove all personnel from the building, effectively calling off the search. A roll call of personnel subsequent to the evacuation order revealed that there were actually six fire fighters missing, all of whom lost their lives that night. In final analysis, it is a lot easier to lead when things are going well, but the true test of a leader comes with unforeseen and difficult events. In my view, his courage and ability to make such a decision under such devastating circumstances form the essence of what being a leader is all about.

Accountability

Yet another area that makes up the foundation of leadership in EMS is accountability. Since the consequences of one's actions or failure to act could be serious, if not life threatening, in EMS, one must be accountable for both one's actions and one's failure to act, regardless of the situation. For providers, duty to act with respect to the care of a patient is clearly defined, but for leaders the definition is more of a grayscale because of the often broad discretion leaders are given in handling day-to-day situations outside the patient care realm. Accountability is one of those things in the field of EMS that extend into one's life outside the job or volunteer agency. For example, the agency's insurance may not allow you to drive company vehicles if you have excessive points on your driver's license. In this situation, not only would your ability to perform day-to-day functions be affected, but so would your authority as a leader. Such disregard for accountability would undermine the guidance you give to a subordinate about his or her driving or any other behavior that may affect his or her performance. You will have lost a large chunk of your earned authority through a lack of personal responsibility and accountability. Taking responsibility for the things that go right as well as the things that go wrong is just one of the many qualities people look for in a leader.

Leadership Qualities

There are many qualities that make leaders effective and perhaps as many that have the ability to make them ineffective. If we think back in our experiences, it is likely we can identify a list of

"If you simply take up the attitude of defending a mistake, there will be no hope of improvement."

–Sir Winston Churchill, British Prime Minister, 1940 to 1945, 1951 to 1955

Leadership Lessons from History

During World War II, Hitler blamed others when things did not go as planned, whereas Churchill readily admitted his mistakes to Parliament and the people of Great Britain. Over the years, Churchill has been widely studied and quoted: "Everyone threw the blame on me. I have noticed that they nearly always do. I suppose it is because they think I shall be able to bear it best." Clearly, he was comfortable with taking responsibility for the good and the bad. As demonstrated by this quote, he was also well aware that others held him responsible. In short, he held himself accountable first and foremost for all successes and failures that occurred under his leadership. In contrast, while Hitler struggled to distance himself from his mistakes, Churchill visited areas of Britain that were ravaged by war. Churchill's actions demonstrated that he accepted responsibility for his country and, in so doing, raised both the morale and the trust of his people.

The reality is that "followers are largely responsible for their own actions" and "leaders are accountable for the performance of their entire department or unit" (Johnson, 2005). This example of Churchill shows that leaders who are accountable for their actions, and the actions of their subordinates, not only are most often successful but also are most often held in higher regard by their followers and those who judge their actions both now and in retrospect.

both effective and ineffective leaders to whom we have reported or whom we have witnessed in action. What was it that made the good leaders effective in our eyes and what was it about the ineffective leaders that placed them in a negative light? Taking stock of the positives and negatives we have experienced allows us to develop our own sense of the impact a leader can have on subordinates, the organization, the field of EMS, and the public.

Like it or not, having a title does not automatically guarantee that others will follow. For a leader to be most effective, he or she must have significantly more positive traits than negative ones. He or she must also realize that sometimes making the unpopular decision because it is right will do more to build credibility as a leader in the long run than doing what may be popular to appease people in the short term. Leaders must set the tone not only in their words but also in their actions. Setting a positive example is just one of the many qualities that distinguish people as leaders and separate the better leaders from the average ones.

If a leader is ineffective or is not trusted, subordinates may not always be strongly committed to following through on the leader's requests. A leader who does not meet the needs or expectations of his or her people often will encounter additional hurdles that do not arise for more effective and

> **Examples of Positive Leadership Qualities**
>
> - Clinical proficiency
> - Honesty
> - Respect for others
> - Integrity
> - Credibility
> - Trustworthiness
> - Vision
> - Empathy
> - Professional demeanor
> - Approachable manner

"The most important action that a leader must take to encourage the building of trust on a team is to demonstrate vulnerability first.**"**

–Patrick Lencioni, National Board of Directors, Make-A-Wish Foundation

Examples of Negative Leadership Qualities

- Dishonesty
- Inflexibility
- Disrespectfulness
- Poor listening skills
- Impatience
- Judgmental nature
- Manipulative behavior
- Small-mindedness
- Bullying
- Cultural insensitivity

respected leaders. In worst-case scenarios, subordinates not only will suffer a lack of enthusiasm for the work and the organization, but they often will try to undermine the leader's ability to lead. To connect with subordinates, a leader must first remember that he or she is human and may well have made some of the very mistakes that subordinates will make. Next, a leader must acknowledge that mistakes are part of life, reveal that he or she, too, has made them, and show that he or she has succeeded either in spite of them or because of them. Leaders who expect their people to "leave it on the field" and take some reasonable risks must do so first. Sometimes a leader will not succeed. When this happens, leaders must let their staff witness this mistake before solving the problem to demonstrate that mistakes are okay. If a leader is successful and shows that he or she is vulnerable, it is more likely that subordinates will take the same risks. Establishing trust is a two-way street that takes time to build but that can be quickly and easily lost. Trust must be both properly built and properly maintained. Additionally, trust must be considered an essential component of every EMS leader's relationship with his or her subordinates, peers, and superiors.

Achieving Positive and Realistic Expectations

Little will diminish a subordinate's self-esteem more than having a boss who doesn't believe in him or her and doubts whether the subordinate is up to the task. Believing in your people, and believing that not only they will do what is right but that they are capable of accomplishing their mission, is vital. Providing them with the support they need and making sure they are aware of your trust in them will provide them with a positive sense of what is expected of them. Every leader must realize, however, that all the belief and support in the world will not guarantee that all subordinates will reach the same heights. Understanding that employees have different strengths and weaknesses will allow you as the leader to recognize that whatever expectations you and your organization have must be not only positive but realistic as well. Understanding that all people have shortcomings and setting positive expectations that are realistic are important parts of leadership. Being prepared to step in and provide the guidance and support necessary to accomplish the job will set up your subordinates, your organization, and you for more success than failure.

"Leaders feel lonely because some decisions can't be shared with a peer or passed up the ladder to a higher position."

–Stephen E. Kohn & Vincent D. O'Connell, authors of *6 Habits of Highly Effective Bosses*

You Are the EMS Leader

Shortly after you begin your shift, one of your subordinates mentions to you that during the previous week, another employee made a comment that the first employee found disturbing. The comment involved possible violent retaliation for a recent departmental decision. The employee alleged to have made the inappropriate comment has been with your organization for less than a year, whereas the employee who brought the matter to your attention has been with your organization for a number of years. The person raising the issue has been known to spread rumors and innuendo, although without ill intent. From the time and place that the comment was alleged to have been made, you know there were at least a handful of others who likely were present and may have information to contribute. Although the employee waited about a week to bring the matter to your attention, no one else has raised the issue with you or, as far as you know, with any other leadership personnel.

1. *How would you initially address the alleged comment by the employee?*

2. *Would you approach the situation differently if the accused were popular and well liked than if he or she were new and didn't have many friends? Why or why not?*

3. *How would the reporting employee's reputation for gossip affect your approach to his concerns?*

Wrap-Up

Chapter Summary

In this chapter, we have uncovered the reality that leadership, in addition to being difficult to define, is much more complicated than just telling others what to do. When making the transition to leadership in EMS, there will be positive examples to emulate and negative ones to overcome. There is an old expression that it is lonely at the top, and this holds true to some degree for every rung of the leadership ladder. As the leader, there will be times you will have to make the unpopular or tough choices that come with the territory. Understanding that leadership is about influencing and motivating others as well as building trust and then being careful not to violate that trust will serve the new and aspiring EMS leader well in his or her career.

Why Their Views Matter: About the Individuals Cited in the Chapter

Mike Adler is a battalion chief and 25-year veteran of the San Bernardino City, California, Fire Department. He instructs and presents programs throughout the country on risk assessment on the fireground, leadership, and communication in the fire service, truck company operations and high-rise operations for smaller fire departments, and command and control on the fireground. He has a BS degree in business administration and an AS degree in fire science.

Larry Boxman has been involved in EMS for more than 25 years. He began his career in the U.S. Air Force and at the time he made the remark quoted here had been working for Metro West Ambulance in Washington County, Oregon, for 12 years, the previous seven as chief of operations.

Mark Burdick began his career as a Glendale fire fighter paramedic in 1983 and rose through the ranks to become fire chief in 2001. He has served as president of the Arizona Fire Chiefs Association. He holds a BS in fire service management and an MS in human resources management. He is also a member of several professional organizations, including the International Association of Fire Chiefs, the National Fire Protection Association, and the International City/County Managers Association. Burdick is an adjunct faculty member at Grand Canyon University. He teaches on several subjects related to the fire service.

Sir Winston Churchill was an officer in the British Army and a Nobel Prize–winning writer who is perhaps best known for his leadership of the United Kingdom during World War II. He served as Prime Minister from 1940 to 1945 and again from 1951 to 1955.

Hans Finzel is the author of *The Top Ten Mistakes Leaders Make* and at the time of its publication was executive director of a church planning and leadership training ministry operating in more than 60 countries worldwide. Previously he had served as a pastor in Long Beach, California, and spent a decade in Vienna, Austria. Dr. Finzel has authored several other books, including *Empowered Leaders*.

Matt Fratus, a 20-year veteran of the fire service, is the deputy chief of the San Bernardino City Fire Department. He spent several years as an instructor of such topics as live-fire training, incident command and tactics, leadership, and fireground decision making. He has a BS degree in fire administration, and he participated in the National Fire Academy's Executive Fire Officer Program.

Rudolph W. Giuliani is the former mayor of New York City who in his final year in office led New York City through the response to and initial recovery from the attacks of September 11, 2001. He is the author of the book *Leadership* and recently was a candidate for president of the United States.

Craig E. Johnson holds a PhD from the University of Denver and is a professor of leadership studies at George Fox University. He teaches graduate and undergraduate courses in leadership, management, ethics, and communication. He is the author of *Meeting the*

Ethical Challenges of Leadership: Casting Light or Shadow. His research is widely published, and he has served on a number of boards of religious and other nonprofit organizations. His work has taken him to the Czech Republic, Brazil, Kenya, Honduras, and New Zealand.

John F. Kennedy was the 35th president of the United States. Before becoming president, he was a lieutenant in the United States Naval Reserve, where he saw duty as the skipper of a PT boat in World War II. He was elected by the people of Massachusetts to serve in both the House of Representatives and the United States Senate.

Stephen E. Kohn is a licensed mental health professional who is a highly respected and experienced executive coach. Before starting his own firm, Work & People Solutions, he served as executive vice president at Paul Sherman & Associates. A graduate of Cornell University and Adelphi University's Graduate School, Kohn's education and his experience provide solid credentials. One of his areas of expertise is motivating leaders to develop methods to maximize the potential of people who report to them. He is coauthor of the book *6 Habits of Highly Effective Bosses.*

Patrick Lencioni is the author of a number of best-selling books, including *The Five Dysfunctions of a Team.* In addition to his work as an author, he consults and speaks to thousands of people each year on topics relating to leadership, teamwork, management, and organization development. He has served on the National Board of Directors for the Make-A-Wish Foundation of America. He is president of The Table Group in San Francisco.

Vince Lombardi, Jr. is the son of the legendary football coach Vince Lombardi, whose uncanny ability to motivate others, along with his insatiable drive for victory, made him the standard against which all leaders in every field are measured. Lombardi Jr has built a successful career in his own right in law, politics, sports, motivational speaking, and writing. He maintained a law practice while serving in the Minnesota legislature and has held executive positions with the Seattle Seahawks, the NFL Management Council, and the United States Football League. He is the author of

The Lombardi Rules, What It Takes to Be #1, and *The Essential Vince Lombardi.*

Vincent D. O'Connell has many years of experience in human resources, consulting, and management. Early in his career, he led an employee assistance program in midwestern Connecticut. He is coauthor of a number of books, including *6 Habits of Highly Effective Bosses* and *The People Management Formula.* He is a graduate of Brown University and received his graduate degree in human resources management from Cornell University.

Jason Rogers has been involved in EMS for 15 years. He began his career in the U.S. Air Force and at the time of his quoted statement had been with Metro West Ambulance for 7 years and served as director of training.

John J. Salka joined the New York City Fire Department in 1979 and rose through the ranks from fire fighter to lieutenant, captain, and battalion chief. As a battalion chief, he leads 30 officers and 150 fire fighters. In addition to his book *First In–Last Out: Leadership Lessons from the New York Fire Department,* he is the author of many articles on fire fighting and leadership techniques. He is a nationally recognized speaker and has been featured at the Worcester Safety and Survival Seminar and a host of other seminars.

John W. Stanko has served as a pastor, administrator, teacher, consultant, and fundraiser. He holds an MS in economics and a doctorate in pastoral ministries. In more than 20 years of ministry, he has taught extensively on time management, life purpose, leadership, and organization throughout the United States and in 20 other countries.

Ralph M. Stogdill is the author and coauthor of seven books and numerous articles of note, including "Personal Factors Associated with Leadership: Survey of Literature," which appeared in the *Journal of Psychology* in 1948. He is professor emeritus at The Ohio State University, Columbus.

Lorin Woolfe has organized and delivered for Manufacturers Hanover Trust, E. F. Hutton, Deloitte, the Institute of Management Accountants, and others. He has served as a specialist in leadership at the American

Management Association and Vice President of Program development for Drake, Beam, Morin (DBM), a globally recognized career management firm. As a student of religion and the Bible for most of his life, he combined his studies with his professional experiences and is the author of *The Bible on Leadership*.

Gary Yukl holds a PhD from the University of California at Berkeley and is a professor at the State University of New York at Albany. He is the author of the text *Leadership in Organizations,* which focuses on effective leadership in organizations through both theory and practice. His book combines theory and his research on leadership, providing an insightful look at the use of power and how its components can influence the behavior of subordinates and peers.

Chapter 2

Leadership Styles

❝The first responsibility of a leader is to define reality. The last is to say 'thank you.' In between, the leader is a servant.❞

—Max DePree

Introduction

There are many leadership styles. In fact, some might argue that there are as many leadership styles as there are leaders. In this chapter, we will discuss a variety of the styles of leadership that have evolved over time. As we look at the ways in which people lead, we will gain an understanding of the advantages and disadvantages of each. Thus, we will expand our knowledge of leadership while simultaneously conducting a self-analysis of our own leadership style that will give us an enriched perspective from which to continue growing as leaders. Self-analysis is important because "if leaders don't know who they are, insecurity and the need to stay on top will cause them to make unwise decisions, thus undermining the leadership they're trying to assert and establish" (Stanko, 2000). By looking at an array of leadership styles, we will better understand who we are as leaders and take away a better understanding of why, in a variety of circumstances, certain styles work and why they don't.

Task and Relationship Behavior

EMS leaders likely will use both task and relationship behavior to some degree every day. Therefore, being clinically proficient as well as having a broad understanding of leadership styles and techniques is essential to being effective in a leadership role in this field. For an EMS leader to provide guidance to a subordinate on a particular task, the leader must be proficient in the skills required to complete that task. Communication with and support for subordinates build the relationship foundation on which a leader can effectively accomplish his or her goals and visions. Understanding that communication and support methods will vary depending on the individual and the relative circumstances will allow the EMS leader to improve his or her effectiveness.

Leaders who use a directive approach tend to be more task oriented, whereas those who engage in more supportive behavior are employee oriented. In EMS, both styles have their place. At the scene of a major incident, for example, a directive approach is likely a better fit for getting the job done. On the other hand, day-to-day operations and interactions with employees may be better handled in a more supportive way.

An EMS leader on the scene of a multiple-vehicle collision is expected to immediately take charge, give a radio report to dispatch, and make prompt decisions about such considerations as scene safety and additional resources. The EMS leader in charge of the incident will then give out the assignments and will expect immediate cooperation. In contrast, back at EMS headquarters, a member of the organization who approaches the EMS leader with a concern about scheduling, for example, likely will expect an opportunity to be heard and that a discussion will take place before a decision is made. The organization member knows that circumstances are different and that his or her issue is not as urgent as the motor vehicle collision, and he or she expects that the EMS leader does as well. By knowing when to simply give an order and when it is more important to listen first, you will build your employees' skills, self-confidence, and trust in you as a leader, and it is likely they will then respond better to both you and the situation when circumstances require a more autocratic approach.

Situational Leadership

As we continue to explore leadership, we will look at some of its many styles. In situational leadership, we will look at how approaching the same situation with different leadership styles can affect its outcome. At the heart of this concept is the understanding that, as Hershey and Blanchard pointed out in their book *The Management of Organizational Behavior*, "it is essential to treat different subordinates differently, and to vary behavior as the situation changes" (as cited in Yukl, 2006). Therefore, before we analyze each of the selected leadership styles, it is important to look at how situational context affects leadership in EMS. I am not suggesting that leaders change who they are or what they believe in response to a given situation—quite the contrary. I am suggesting that the same leadership approach that would serve an EMS leader well in the field likely would not work well when handling a citizen's complaint about the manner in which he was treated or during a budget meeting with the city manager. Having an understanding of the situation and the people involved and modifying your approach to get the job done without compromising yourself, your organization, or anyone's safety in the process allows leaders to accomplish the best results regardless of the circumstances.

> **"**A good leader will find him- or herself switching instinctively between styles according to the people and work they are dealing with.**"**
>
> –James Manktelow, Founder and CEO of Mind Tools

Autocratic Leadership

In the autocratic leadership style, the leader essentially has complete power. As discussed earlier, in EMS and other emergency services, this style of leadership is often used in an operational setting during emergencies. This style provides little opportunity for suggestions or input from subordinates. Outside the emergency scene, and even on occasion at the emergency scene, people will balk at this approach. In EMS, overuse or inappropriate use of the autocratic approach could lead to poor morale, absenteeism, and high turnover. It is important to remember that EMS personnel are professionals. They are taught to think and act independently, and, although they understand chain-of-command, they expect and deserve to be treated with respect.

However, providing specific direction and close monitoring may be required in some cases, such as those involving a new or inexperienced provider, or even an experienced provider who is new to your agency and needs guidance on policies and procedures.

When used correctly, autocratic leadership can be very effective. However, when overused or used incorrectly, it can lead to misunderstandings, morale issues, and even fear. Even in the military, the autocratic approach isn't always as simple as it is portrayed in the movies and on television. Autocratic leadership is just one of many approaches an EMS leader can employ. Remember the old expression about "everything in moderation."

Transactional Leadership

Transactional leadership is more of a management style, focusing on supervision and performance, reward and punishment. Positive results are rewarded, whereas less-than-desired results are reprimanded or punished. Too often, leaders in all fields focus more on punishment than reward. For this approach to be effective in EMS, the leader must understand the difference between "corrective" and "disciplinary" action. There are times when a correction is required, such as when an individual makes a mistake. These instances should not be confused with inappropriate behavior that requires discipline, such as harassment or a blatant violation of policy. Taking the time to acknowledge proper behavior will set the tone and perhaps make the times when corrective or disciplinary action are necessary less frequent.

People-Oriented (Servant) Leadership

A former organizational development consultant at the University of California, Berkeley, wrote, "If I feel my boss is looking out for me, has my interests and goals in mind, and can help me optimize my potential, chances are I bring more loyalty and spirit to my work" (McManus, 2006). With an emphasis on organizing and developing their people, those leaders who are more people oriented will likely find their greatest success in the kinds of coaching and mentoring activities that can be used for both subordinate development and team building. Servant leadership is a form of people-oriented leadership that was first alluded to by Robert Greenleaf in the 1970s. At the core of servant leadership is the concept that "when someone, at any level within an organization, leads simply by virtue of meeting the needs of his or her team, he or she is described as a servant leader" (Manktelow, 2003). Additionally, servant leadership requires the servant leader to empower followers while simultaneously standing up for what is right.

Participative Leadership

Lending itself to inclusion and buy-in of the organization's stakeholders, participative leadership, also known as democratic leadership, has its strengths in allowing both positive and negative input on an idea before it is implemented. This style requires a leader to be a good listener while allowing subordinates to contribute ideas and opinions to shape the future of their organization. Often in EMS and other organizations, new policies are created by the top officials or leaders, but are then implemented by their employees. Occasionally, the employees discover unforeseen flaws that were not addressed properly by their superiors. In the short term, including input from key personnel in the discussion of a new policy is a great use of participative leadership because it identifies areas the leader may not have seen and creates an opportunity to begin to develop the influence that will ease the policy's eventual implementation. In the long run, including more people in the process will improve morale and create a sense of ownership in the organization.

Leadership Through the Hollywood Lens

The movie *Crimson Tide* (Scott, 1995) illustrates a number of lessons about leadership styles. The film depicts the civil instability of Russia during the Cold War period, and Russian rebels have taken over a nuclear missile site. In response, the *USS Alabama*, a United States Navy nuclear submarine, is deployed to secure a strategic position from which it can launch a preemptive strike should the Russians begin fueling the missiles in preparation for a strike against the United States. When his executive officer (second in command) is sidelined by appendicitis, Captain Ramsey (played by Gene Hackman), the commanding officer of the *USS Alabama*, is forced to select an interim executive officer before the submarine departs on this urgent mission. Initially, Captain Ramsey tries to mentor his new executive officer with words of encouragement and advice. As time goes on, instead of complementing one another's strengths and weaknesses, their differences in leadership style and vision leave them at odds.

Captain Ramsey is more of an autocratic leader who relies heavily on both his legal and his earned authority. Part of his style is to challenge his officers and crew to be certain they are as prepared as possible for a crisis. For example, shortly after a fire on board the submarine is contained, Ramsey calls for a weapons system readiness drill. In doing so, he takes advantage of the existing chaos to force his officers and crew to meet the challenge of balancing multiple urgent issues simultaneously. Because most of the crew had not had a chance to wind down from the emotions and responsibilities generated by the fire, Captain Ramsey sees the moment as an opportunity to challenge his crew even further by calling the drill immediately after the fire.

His new executive officer, Lieutenant Commander Hunter (Denzel Washington), on the other hand, has a leadership style that in many ways is the opposite of Captain Ramsey's. In a clear demonstration of their different approaches, Lieutenant Commander Hunter tells Captain Ramsey that he feels the men were "on edge" and in need of "a pat on the back" as a means of encouragement during a stressful time. Evidently, Lieutenant Commander Hunter felt that the tension of the threat of impending nuclear war was taking its toll on morale and that a few words of appreciation from the commanding officer would help improve the situation. However, although Captain Ramsey recognizes that Lieutenant Commander Hunter has a better grasp of the crew's mentality, Ramsey feels that their anxiety is a sign of weakness, and he chastises the men by stating that anyone who is not up to the job can simply leave the ship. This is unrealistic because the submarine is hundreds of feet under the sea, but it clearly illustrates Captain Ramsey's old-school bravado style of leadership.

The movie concludes with the findings of an investigation into the behavior of both Ramsey and Hunter. Ultimately, the investigation recognizes their differences in style and acknowledges that they were both right and both wrong in how they handled the situation. Note that although both were faulted for not communicating and working out their differences, neither was faulted for his leadership style. Additionally, as the more senior leader, Captain Ramsey took the brunt of the criticism and responsibility. In the film and in the real world, the more senior your position, the more responsibility and ownership of a situation you must take.

> *"Involvement in decision-making improves the understanding of the issues involved by those who must carry out the decisions."*
>
> –David Straker, principle consultant and author of Changingminds.org

Charismatic Leadership

A charismatic leader uses his or her enthusiasm and energy to motivate others. Often those who follow the charismatic leader credit their success more to the leader's presence than to their own hard work, which was motivated by the leader in the first place. At times, charismatic leaders tend to believe more in themselves than in their people. When both subordinates and the leader put much of the credit for success on the charismatic leader's presence, it is important that those who invoke this style of leadership consider long-term commitments to their organizations because their departure will very likely create a leadership vacuum.

Laissez-Faire Leadership

"Laissez-faire" means to "leave it be." This is a hands-off macro-leadership approach in which the leader simply provides broad direction followed by periodic monitoring and feedback. It is most effective for dealing with subordinates who are both proficient at their positions and independently motivated to do their jobs and accomplish the goals of the organization. On the flip side, it has been used to refer to leaders who do not provide sufficient supervision or guidance to their personnel.

Bureaucratic Leadership

Bureaucratic or by-the-book leadership is not foreign to EMS. In fact, it is probably seen most often in the policies and standing orders issued by management and medical directors. The expectation of a bureaucratic leader is that the policies or standing orders will be followed exactly as

Leadership Lessons from History

Ronald Reagan was considered a visionary by Pete du Pont, who characterized him as "a believer in bringing everyone around the table to accomplish mutual goals" (as cited in Taranto and Leo, 2005). His successor, Bill Clinton, was more the charismatic type whose presidency was described by Paul Johnson (as cited in Taranto & Leo, 2005) as "one of the longest periods of laissez-faire in U.S. History." In looking at the variety of traits of our past presidents, we can see that each had a very different style of doing the same important job. Each was successful in many ways and each made his share of mistakes. Faulkner said, "Don't try to be better than your predecessors or contemporaries—try to be better than yourself" (as cited in Haid, 2005). Each individual brings a unique perspective, style, and ability to his or her position. What history teaches us is that it is important to realize that there is no single mold for the ideal EMS leader.

written. Bruce Evans, Chief of EMS with the North Las Vegas Fire Department and an adjunct faculty member with the National Fire Academy, puts it into perspective when he explains that "the pre-hospital world will be required to put in place procedures, policies, and practices that will be subject to the scrutiny of evidence-based medicine and require a return on investment." In the face of increased public and peer scrutiny, the challenge of this style of leadership in EMS is that often the situations encountered by personnel do not exactly match the "book" because, despite the best efforts, not every scenario can be anticipated precisely.

Transformational Leadership

Transformational leadership is centered on the connection between leaders and followers. According to Van Wagner (2007), "these leaders motivate and inspire people by helping group members see the importance and higher good of the task." These leaders not only look at group performance, they encourage individual success and growth. Additionally, most transformational leaders have high moral and ethical standards that they impart to their people through example.

The Connection Between Leadership and Followership

Almost every leader is also a follower. Whether to a supervisor or manager, a board of directors or a municipal council, the EMS leader is answerable or accountable to someone. Therefore, all leaders are also followers and, according to Gary Yukl, a professor at the State University of New York at Albany and the author of *Leadership in Organizations*, "to be effective in both roles simultaneously, it is important to find a way to integrate them."

> **"**Leadership style is how you behave when you are trying to influence the performance of someone else.**"**
>
> –Ken Blanchard, author of *Leadership and the One Minute Manager*

You Are the EMS Leader

You are an EMS shift supervisor, and your superiors bring to your attention a complaint that one of your people provided poor customer service the day before. Coincidentally, you had spoken with this person recently about his behavior in a similar matter. You believe that this counseling session was productive and that the individual should now be given an opportunity to correct his behavior before further action is considered. However, your superior clearly wants you to take written disciplinary action because although there was only one complaint, there were multiple occurrences of poor behavior.

1. *Do you agree or disagree with your superior in this case? Why or why not?*

2. *If you disagree with your superior, how would you proceed? Why?*

3. *Given that you already spoke with the individual about his behavior, how do you think he and the rest of the staff will respond if you take written disciplinary action now?*

4. *List the benefits and pitfalls of each approach as they affect you as a leader, the individual in question, and the organization as a whole.*

Wrap-Up

Chapter Summary

Several different leadership styles were discussed in this chapter. In today's society, there is no one best approach for every person and situation. Therefore, leaders must take stock of their choices and self-reflect after both good days and bad. By understanding that competent subordinates require a different approach than less-committed employees, a leader will be successful. By accepting that there are many ways to accomplish the same objectives and by being open to a variety of approaches, the EMS leader likely will have a more successful career.

Why Their Views Matter: About the Individuals Cited in the Chapter

Ken Blanchard is the author of *Leadership and the One Minute Manager* as well as coauthor of *The One Minute Manager* and a number of other books on topics relating to leadership, management, and motivation. He has served as a consultant for a number of top corporations and is well known as a dynamic teacher and speaker. He is a polished storyteller with a knack for making the seemingly complex easy to understand. He received his BA and his PhD from Cornell University, where he is a visiting lecturer and a trustee emeritus.

Max DePree is the author of the book *Leadership Is an Art*. He served as CEO of the Herman Miller office furniture company and was a laureate of the American National Business Hall of Fame. He has also written a number of other books on leadership, including *Leadership Jazz* and *Leading Without Power: Finding Hope in Serving Community*.

Pete du Pont has served as a state legislator, U.S. Congressman, and governor and in 1988 was a Republican candidate for president of the United States. He began his political career in 1968 with his election to the House of Representatives of the Delaware General Assembly. He served for 6 years (1971–1977) in the U.S. House of Representatives. He was a member of the Foreign Affairs Committee and in 1975 was picked by *Time* magazine as one of America's "200 Faces for the Future."

Bruce Evans is the EMS chief of the North Las Vegas (Nevada) Fire Department. He is also the fire science program coordinator at the Community College of Southern Nevada and an adjunct faculty member for the National Fire Academy's EMS and injury prevention courses. He has an associate's degree in fire management and an MS degree in public administration.

William Faulkner was awarded the Nobel Prize in Literature in 1949 and is widely considered one of the most influential writers of the 20th century. Among his many works are 13 novels and numerous short stories. He was also a published poet and an occasional screenwriter.

Robert K. Greenleaf is widely considered the founder of the modern servant leadership movement. He graduated from Carleton College in Minnesota. He spent 20 years researching management, development, and education and in 1964 founded the Center for Applied Ethics. He is the author of many works on servant leadership, including *The Institution as Servant*, *The Leadership Crisis: A Message for College and University Faculty*, and *Teacher as Servant*. After his death in 1990, the Center for Applied Ethics was renamed the Robert K. Greenleaf Center, and a number of posthumous essay collections have been published.

Paul Johnson is the author of *Art: A New History* as well as the section on William Jefferson Clinton in the book *Presidential Leadership: Rating the Best and the Worst in the White House*. He attended Stonyhurst College and Magdalen College and has enjoyed a successful career as a journalist, historian, speechwriter, and author. He served as an advisor to British Prime Minister Margaret Thatcher and was honored in 2006 by President George W. Bush with the Presidential Medal of Freedom.

James Manktelow is the founder and CEO of Mind Tools, an organization whose mission is to help people around the world learn the practical skills needed to excel in their careers. Since its inception, Mind Tools has become a popular and frequently visited career skills website.

Patty McManus has provided leadership and organization development consulting to organizations for nearly 20 years. She has focused on developing collaborative change processes and skill in for-profit, public, and nonprofit sectors. She served as an internal organizational development consultant at the University of California at Berkeley, Kaiser Permanente, and Apple Computer. She has an MS degree in industrial and organizational psychology from San Francisco State University.

John W. Stanko has served as a pastor, administrator, teacher, consultant, and fundraiser. He holds an MS degree in economics and a doctorate in pastoral ministries. In more than 20 years of ministry, he has taught extensively on time management, life purpose, leadership, and organization throughout the United States and in 20 other countries.

David Straker is the principal consultant and author of the website changingminds.org. He has a long background in counseling, therapy, marketing, sales, education, international management, and consulting.

Kendra Van Wagner holds a BS degree in psychology from Idaho State University and has additional coursework in chemical addictions and case management. She is currently completing her MS degree in education with an emphasis in educational technology. She is also a writer specializing in psychology, child development, and education. She has written about diverse topics in psychology, including personality, social behavior, child therapy, and research methods.

Gary Yukl holds a PhD from the University of California at Berkeley and is a professor at the State University of New York at Albany. He is the author of the text *Leadership in Organizations*, which focuses on effective leadership in organizations through both theory and practice. His book combines theory and his research on leadership, providing an insightful look at the use of power and how its components can influence the behavior of subordinates and peers.

Chapter 3

The Impact of Ethics on Leadership

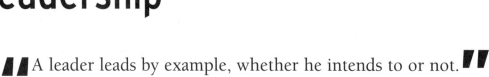

❚❚ A leader leads by example, whether he intends to or not. **❚❚**

—Anonymous

Introduction

The topic of ethics is stressed early in EMS provider training and includes confidentiality, honesty in reporting, and respect for patients, coworkers, and the public at large. For leaders in EMS, ethics and ethical behavior take on great importance. Leaders in EMS must not only be concerned with what those in the EMS profession perceive as ethical behavior, but they must also consider the perceptions and expectations of the public.

When discussions of ethics take place, the topics of values, morals, and integrity often are included or at least considered by those involved in the dialogue. As EMS providers, we are taught not to impose our values on our patients and our partners. For example, we must not judge how others live when we arrive at their homes in their time of need. If a home is simply a bit messy by our standards, that is the person's business. If the home is obviously unsanitary, then our observations as professionals are shared appropriately with those who can provide assistance. Ethically, and in many states legally, we have an obligation to report health risks and potential safety hazards. In the field as EMS providers, our honesty and integrity are front and center every day and in every home and situation we encounter. As EMS leaders, we must realize that our ethics, values, morals, and integrity will face new and evolving challenges beyond those we faced as providers.

"From an EMS standpoint, ethics are associated with what the profession of EMS providers deems proper or fitting conduct."

–Andrew N. Pollak, series editor of *Emergency Care and Transportation of the Sick and Injured*, Ninth Edition

Ethical Leadership

In Chapter 1, we explored the virtual impossibility of creating a single definition for the term "leadership." Through this exploration, however, we gained the understanding that there can and will be times as leaders when we will encounter situations in which something cannot be concretely or otherwise clearly defined. According to Craig E. Johnson, professor of leadership studies at George Fox University and author of the book *Meeting the Ethical Challenges of Leadership*, "the term ethics refers to judgments about whether human behavior is right or wrong." With this in mind, we must explore both the human side of ethical leadership and whether the simple test of right or wrong can be applied to it.

In defining and evaluating ethical leadership, we must consider both the individual leader and the particular context within which that leader makes a decision or takes an action. In the same situation, for example, a leader with a reputation for fairness and integrity likely would be judged differently from one whose character may be in question. It should also be noted that "the final evaluation can be influenced as much by the qualities of the judge as by the qualities of the leader" (Yukl, 2006). In other words, sometimes no matter how beyond reproach a leader may be, others may see the leader in a less flattering light because of their own experiences and perspectives rather than the integrity of the leader. Understanding that decision-making biases affect us all will go a long way toward the practice of ethical leadership.

> ### Language of Leadership
>
> - **Ethics**—A system or set of moral principles
> - **Morals**—Pertaining to or concerned with the principles of right conduct or the distinction between right and wrong
> - **Values**—The abstract concepts of what is right, worthwhile, or desirable; principles or standards
> - **Integrity**—Uncompromising adherence to moral and ethical principles; soundness of moral character; honesty

Honesty and Integrity

Leaders expect their subordinates to be honest and to have a foundation of integrity on which their trust is placed. Subordinates have the same if not a higher expectation of their leaders. The capacity to trust and be trusted is the mortar that holds this foundation together. All too often we see examples of the ends justifying the means, yet Lorin Woolfe, a former specialist in the area of leadership at the American Management Association and author of *The Bible on Leadership: From Moses to Matthew—Management Lessons for Contemporary Leaders*, said it best: "it doesn't matter how noble or worthwhile your cause, if you haven't earned people's trust by constantly keeping your word and being true to your values people won't follow you too far" (Woolfe, 2002). If a subordinate sees a leader bending or breaking the rules and not setting a good example, this diminishes the leader's ability to lead and establishes a norm for subordinates to emulate. One must realize that there is a big difference between a leader who exercises the discretion of the position and a leader who compromises his or her integrity under the cloak of discretion.

> **"**You can no longer lead by virtue of having more information than anyone else, by hiding secrets, or relying on deference to the authority of your job title or by projecting a fake you as uber-leader.**"**
>
> –Phil Dourado & Phil Blackburn, coauthors of *Seven Secrets of Inspired Leaders*

You Are the EMS Leader

In your role as an EMS supervisor or officer, you receive a complaint alleging maliciously inappropriate behavior by one of your subordinates. The subordinate allegedly altered records to make the person lodging the complaint look and perhaps feel incompetent. You listen to the complaint and request that the facts—dates, times, and any other pertinent information—be documented to the best of the reporting party's ability. You inform the reporting party that you will look into the matter and ask that he or she refrain from discussing it with others pending the outcome of the investigation.

During the course of the investigation, you have occasion to review numerous records that span a period of weeks and discover that there is merit to the concerns of the employee who brought the matter to your attention. However, while investigating the concerns of malicious inappropriate behavior, you also inadvertently discover a few mistakes, with no apparent ill intent, made by both the reporting party and others. The mistakes you discover pale in comparison to the changes made to the records, but still they are mistakes that indicate a possible need for remediation.

You handle the initial matter in accordance with agency disciplinary and corrective action policy and take the appropriate steps to mitigate the situation. This leaves the dilemma of how to handle the other mistakes you inadvertently discovered in the course of your investigation into the unrelated inappropriate behavior.

1. *Since the mistakes were minor in comparison to the initial complaint and would not have otherwise been discovered, would it be appropriate to look past them this time because of how they were discovered? Why or why not?*

2. *If you chose not to look past the inadvertently discovered mistakes by others in your investigation of the alleged wrongdoing, describe the general approach you would take to address the mistakes in contrast to the inappropriate behavior.*

Impact of the Leader's Character

In Chapter 1, we discussed the three types of authority: legal, moral, and earned. As we move further into the discussion of leadership, and in particular the role of ethics as it relates to one's ability to lead, we should consider that two of the factors that affect authority are centered on ethics, in particular, the ethical actions and decisions of the leaders themselves.

Aspiring, new, and even long-time leaders in EMS must continually endeavor to maintain an "above-reproach" persona in everything they do. Granted, even the best of leaders will make mistakes. However, when mistakes are made, one will be judged, not only in the context of the mistake, but also in the context of one's reputation, and both will affect the short- and long-term effects of the leader's continued ability to effectively lead. Senator John McCain and Mark Salter, in their book *Character is Destiny*, summed it up like this: "others can encourage you to make the right choices or discourage you, but you choose." The people around you may not always agree with your decisions as a leader, but if they have trust in your character and believe that your decision was made for the right reason and not because of pressure from others or self-interest, they will respect you. Through ethical behavior, you will have both done what you believed was right in the various situations you face and increased your moral and earned authority for the future in the process.

> ## Language of Leadership
>
> - **Ethical Behavior**—Behavior judged as good, right, just, honorable, and praiseworthy
> - **Unethical Behavior**—Behavior judged to be wrong, unjust, dishonorable, or failing to meet an obligation
>
> ---
>
> *Source: Organizational Behavior* (Champoux, 2006).

Encouraging Ethical Behavior Versus Discouraging Unethical Behavior

It has been said that actions speak louder than words, and most would agree that this premise has merit. By walking the walk and not just talking the talk, a leader will go a long way toward setting a high standard of behavior and creating an environment of respect. Additionally, it is perhaps more important to focus on, point out, and reward ethical behavior than it is to simply reprimand or discipline inappropriate or improper behavior. EMS leaders' own actions should provide the example for others to follow. In fact, "it is essential for integrity of action that your relationships be founded on mutual trust and confidence" (Drewry, 2004). Additionally, taking a proactive and positive approach will build trust and improve compliance with expected behavior. Too often, however, there is a tendency to focus on negative consequences of improper behavior, resulting in an environment of fear and diminished trust. With the positive approach, improper behavior is discouraged before it happens. In contrast, the approach of opposing and punishing unethical behavior often is used after the improper behavior has already occurred, and, even before any punitive measures are taken, the damage has already been done. Clearly, promoting ethics through a positive environment is the more desirable approach and perhaps one that minimizes and eliminates ethical lapses and their inherent damage before they occur.

> **"**A person who does something correctly and receives a positive response will most likely continue that desired behavior.**"**
>
> –Ken Blanchard, author of *Leadership and the One Minute Manger*

Leadership Through the Hollywood Lens

During the first season of the television series "Rescue Me," a female firefighter named Laura (played by Diane Farr) is assigned to the Ladder 62 firehouse. In accordance with policy, she is provided with separate sleeping quarters and a private bathroom. As she attempts to fit in, she is consistently rejected by the other members of the fire company, and, eventually, her private bathroom becomes the scene of a practical joke by the male personnel. She brings the matter to the attention of Battalion Chief Jerry Reilly (Jack McGee), who approaches the crew with her concerns. As she leaves the room, Chief Reilly scolds, "there are limits to what's funny." Once she is out of earshot, he proceeds to tell the crew in great detail that he was responsible for the incident. As the chief walks out and the crew laughs, Lieutenant Shea (John Scurti) further supports the chief's behavior: "That, gentlemen, is why he wears the white shirt."

Ethics and ethical behavior are often a gray area. Nevertheless, these kinds of situations can serve as opportunities to separate what is popular from what is proper. In this case, the chief led Laura to believe that he did not condone the inappropriate behavior. Yet, his admission to the crew sent the message that it was okay to ignore both policy and basic respect for a coworker. "Those with little courage fold in the face of adversity; those with great courage only find their courage magnified when confronted with difficulties" (Woolfe, 2002). Clearly, Chief Reilly's behavior showed that it was more important to him to stay in favor with the crew than to put a stop to the inappropriate behavior toward Laura. His behavior portrayed a leader with little courage, and ultimately, his actions served to discourage rather than encourage ethical behavior.

Discrimination and Harassment

When you are a leader, ignoring others' inappropriate actions in the workplace is not an option. While those without official positions are guided mostly by their own moral compass in such situations, those in official positions have a legal and an ethical obligation to mitigate any situations they witness. Surely they have the same, if not stronger, obligation not to participate in the behavior. Perhaps the best advice I have heard comes from "Winnie" Maggiore, a paramedic and attorney specializing in EMS-related law. She put it like this: "To avoid injuries and/or lawsuits resulting from hazing, horseplay, and harassment, EMS managers and line officers must take a strict stand against abusive actions." Remembering her advice, consider the reality that each time a subordinate sees a superior ignore discrimination or harassment, or worse yet, participates in the behavior, the message to the subordinate is that this action is acceptable. Either way, the leader, the organization, and the victims all suffer the consequences. Although it is important for agencies to have strong policies that prohibit inappropriate behavior, it is even more important that, through their actions, the leaders within the organization establish and maintain an atmosphere of respect so that punitive measures in the policy never have to be invoked.

Objective Versus Subjective Ethics

When we think of judging ethical behavior and decisions, we think of a barometer of solely right and wrong. However, is it really that simple? In 2004, Peter Vernezze and Richard Greene wrote the book *The Sopranos and Philosophy*. Both are accomplished professors and prolific writers, and their take is that "moral claims are true or false in the same way as clear matters of fact like the earth is round." At the same time, they realize that on the other side of the argument are those who believe that "the truth or falsity of moral claims depends not on some alleged objective fact of the matter about the act, but rather on the feelings, beliefs, or attitudes of the person passing the judgment." There will be times when we as leaders pass judgment and other times when the judgment will be passed on us, just like in patient assessment there are objective observations as well as subjective ones.

Taking an example from patient care, I think we will all agree that committing battery (the act of touching someone without their consent) against a patient would be considered both improper and illegal. Therefore, one would think this would be an example of clear-cut right and wrong. Yet, as EMS providers, we all know that in the case of a combative patient, it is considered acceptable to "use restraints only to protect yourself or others from bodily harm or to prevent the patient from causing injury to himself or herself," provided that we "use the minimum force necessary" (Browner, Pollak, & Gupton, 2002). Several questions often are raised in such situations:

- Was the patient really a threat to himself or herself or to others?
- How much force is sufficient and how much is too much?
- Did the EMTs and paramedics exhaust every option before restraining someone against his or her will?

From this example, we can see that although there are times when something may appear to be as simple as right and wrong, there often will be times when a different perspective will turn the objective into the subjective. Most will agree that subjective analysis of what we in EMS do is not new to us. However, as leaders we must realize more acutely how important ethically sound decisions are on all levels. We as leaders not only will be judged for our own decisions, but we will also be held responsible for the decisions of our subordinates.

In looking at both the objective and subjective views of ethical and other decisions a leader makes, let's not forget the old adage that hindsight is 20/20. The challenge facing EMS leaders is that the decisions we make, while often judged retrospectively by myriad people with a wide range of experiences and biases, must be made in the present under often stressful and critical circumstances. It is also important to remember that when our decisions and actions are judged by others, they will be scrutinized as much through the filter of their subjective beliefs as by a purely objective right-versus-wrong approach.

Legal Issues

Understanding the legal system as it relates to EMS is important to providers and leaders alike. When legal issues are covered during EMT and paramedic training, topics like scope of practice,

"It is often helpful to think what you would expect of medical professionals if the patient were a member of your own family."

–Mark C. Henry & Edward R. Stapleton, coauthors of *EMT Prehospital Care*, Third edition

Leadership Lessons from History

Throughout history, the actions and statements of leaders around the country and the world have been used to assess their credibility and ability to lead. Lorin Woolfe, author of *Leadership Secrets of the Bible*, reminds us that "in recent years, we have been treated to leaders like Bill Clinton asking interrogators to clarify the meaning of the word 'is' and Bill Gates questioning the meaning of the word 'concerned.'" However, questioning the integrity and ethical compasses of our leaders is not new. If we look back just a few decades further, we find President Gerald Ford's decision to pardon Richard Nixon for unethical and illegal activities. Some would argue that his decision halted the judicial process and allowed former President Nixon to escape prosecution. Some speculated that Ford traded a pardon for the presidency. Still others argued that President Ford's decision allowed the country to move past the Nixon years and begin to heal; Caroline Kennedy, president of the John F. Kennedy Library Foundation, wrote of Ford that his "ambition for the country was larger than his own ambition" in her book *Profiles in Courage for Our Time*. In the aftermath of his decision, however, President Ford's approval went from 71% to 49% and the pardon likely contributed to his loss in the presidential election of 1976.

As a leader in EMS, your actions and decisions will be judged by others every day. Sometimes you will be judged fairly and given the benefit of the doubt, and at other times you will be the victim of a rushed judgment. Given that "honesty and integrity pay off long-term, though they may involve losses and sacrifices short term" (Woolfe, 2002), it is important that your ethical compass is not askew. If you make decisions with integrity of purpose that are ethically sound and not unduly biased, you may occasionally encounter those who balk at your decisions, but in the long run you will be judged as a fair and honest leader and have the satisfaction of a clear conscience. It is this type of leader that we all should strive to be and that people everywhere desire to follow.

standard of care, duty to act, abandonment, and negligence are at the core of the discussion. When you are an EMS leader, these topics are still part of your everyday considerations; however, topics like discrimination, harassment, and hostile work environment, and many others, are now added with as much and at times even more, emphasis. Because even an entire chapter in this book would not provide the foundation of material that an EMS leader needs to begin to understand the legal system in America as it relates to EMS, my strong recommendation is that you add *EMS and the Law*, another in the AAOS EMS Continuing Education Series published by Jones and Bartlett Publishers, to your EMS leadership reading list and keep it handy for reference. In their book, Jacob L. Hafter and Victoria L. Fedor, who are both attorneys as well as EMS providers, did an outstanding job in creating a primer for everyone in EMS, in particular for the EMS leader. I have found that leaders need not have all the answers on the tips of their tongues. Instead, they must surround themselves with good people and know how to put their hands on the information and resources they need. Just as the public and others look to us in their time of medical need because we are the professionals with the requisite background, so too should we not hesitate to look to others with the expertise required to address a particular concern we may have in our roles as leaders.

Creating an Ethical Organizational Climate

From a leadership perspective, establishing and maintaining an ethical culture requires using the current culture of the organization as a starting point from which to determine where the organization is ethically, where it needs to go, and how to get it there successfully. Ethical behavior cannot be imposed by force, policy, or codes of ethics. In fact, "moral philosophers agree that ethical behavior happens because a person freely believes it is the right way to behave" (Champoux, 2006). However, ethical behavior can be encouraged, improved, and maintained by using these and other tools, including a positive ethical example set by the leaders of the organization.

Historically, "U.S. organizations rely heavily on rules applied equally to all people," whereas "organizations in other countries rely more on shared values and a sense of obligation to other people or organizations" (Vogel, as cited in Champoux, 2006). Encouraging participation by the organization's membership will go a long way in establishing and maintaining policies, codes, and behaviors that everyone will believe in and abide by. If, for example, staff members are part of the committee that writes the organization's code of ethics or have input into the ethical and behavioral policies or perhaps an opportunity to review them and provide feedback before implementation, the likelihood that they will take ownership of the policies increases significantly. Perhaps blending our country's focus on policies that apply equally to all and the lessons from abroad that environments with shared values have proved effective can result in a powerful tool for leaders to use to establish and maintain not only ethically sound organizations, but, better still, organizations centered on mutual respect.

Wrap-Up

Chapter Summary

In this chapter, we have discussed and defined ethics and explored the effect of the integrity of leaders, as well as the biases of those who judge them, on how a leader is perceived and how effective he or she is in the leadership position. We also discussed the importance of setting a positive example and encouraging positive behavior rather than discouraging negative behavior. Finally, we looked at the role of the leader and the followers in developing and maintaining an organizational culture that is free of harassment and has its foundations in respect and shared values.

Why Their Views Matter: About the Individuals Cited in the Chapter

Phil Blackburn is cofounder of the Inspired Leaders Network and one of the originators of the United Kingdom's Business Link network. He has been CEO of the government agency charged with economic development in West London and is currently chairman of Inspired Movies, a feature film production company. In addition to coauthoring *Seven Secrets of Inspired Leaders*, he has written books on innovation and economic growth.

Ken Blanchard is the author of *Leadership and the One Minute Manager* as well as coauthor of *The One Minute Manager* and a number of other books on topics relating to leadership, management, and motivation. He has served as a consultant for a number of top corporations and is well known as a dynamic teacher and speaker. He is a polished storyteller with a knack for making the seemingly complex easy to understand. He received his BA degree and his PhD from Cornell University, where he is a visiting lecturer and a trustee emeritus.

Joseph E. Champoux received his PhD from the Graduate School of Management at the University of California, Irvine, with an emphasis in organizational theory, organizational behavior, and research methodology. In addition to serving as a professor of management at the University of New Mexico, Dr. Champoux is a Contributing Scholar at Walden University and has been a visiting professor at numerous colleges and universities in France, the Netherlands, and Austria.

Phil Dourado is a writer, editor, and analyst who has written for a wide range of newspapers and magazines on both sides of the Atlantic, including the *New Statesman*, the *New Scientist, GQ*, and the *Daily Telegraph*. He is a chief storyteller of the Inspired Leaders Network.

Douglas L. Drewry is the author of numerous books, such as *Successful Leadership Today, The Chief Petty Officer's Manual*, and *The Definitive Performance Writing Guide*.

Richard Greene is an assistant professor of philosophy at Weber State University. He received his PhD in philosophy from the University of California, Santa Barbara. He has published papers in epistemology, metaphysics, and ethics.

Mark C. Henry is coauthor of *EMT Prehospital Care*, third edition, and is professor and chairman of the Department of Emergency Medicine at the School of Medicine of the State University of New York, Stony Brook.

Craig E. Johnson holds a PhD from the University of Denver and is a professor of leadership studies at George Fox University. He teaches graduate and undergraduate courses in leadership, management, ethics, and communication. He is the author of *Meeting the Ethical Challenges of Leadership: Casting Light or Shadow*. His research is widely published, and he has served on a number of boards of religious and other nonprofit organizations. His work has taken him to the Czech Republic, Brazil, Kenya, Honduras, and New Zealand.

Caroline Kennedy is the editor of the *New York Times* bestseller *The Best-Loved Poems of Jacqueline Kennedy Onassis* and coauthor of *The Right to Privacy* and *In Our Defense: The Bill of Rights in Action*. She serves as president of the John F. Kennedy Library Foundation. She also edited and introduced the book *Profiles in Courage for Our Time*, which tells the stories of numerous public servants who have taken a stand in the face of public opinion or political pressure.

W. Ann "Winnie" Maggiore has served as a paramedic, assistant fire chief, state EMS administrator, and criminal prosecutor during her career. She is a practicing attorney who defends physicians, dentists, nurses, law enforcement, and EMS personnel while continuing to volunteer as a paramedic in rural New Mexico. Additionally, she frequently writes on EMS issues and speaks at national conferences. She holds a faculty appointment at the University of New Mexico School of Medicine.

John McCain was elected to the U.S. Senate in 1986 after a career in the U.S. Navy and two terms in the U.S. House of Representatives. In 2008, he was the U.S. Republican presidential nominee and lost to democratic nominee Barack Obama.

Andrew N. Pollak has been active in EMS activities since 1980, when he started as a volunteer fire fighter and first responder. During his career he has served as an EMT-A, an EMT-Paramedic, and a flight physician with a hospital-based aeromedical ambulance service. He is an attending orthopaedic trauma surgeon at the R. Adams Cowley Shock Trauma Center in Baltimore, Maryland. He remains active in EMS as a fire surgeon for the Baltimore County Fire Department and as an educator and administrator.

Mark Salter has worked on Senator John McCain's staff for more than 15 years and together they have written four books, *Faith of My Fathers*, *Worth Fighting For*, *Why Courage Matters*, and *Character Is Destiny*.

Edward R. Stapleton is coauthor of *EMT Prehospital Care*, third edition, and associate professor of clinical emergency medicine as well as director of prehospital education in the Department of Emergency Medicine at the State University of New York, Stony Brook.

Peter J. Vernezze is an associate professor of philosophy at Weber State University in Ogden, Utah. He received his PhD from the University of Washington. He is the author of *Don't Worry, Be Stoic: Ancient Wisdom for Troubled Times*.

David Vogel received his BA degree from Queens College and his PhD from the Department of Politics at Princeton University. He has authored numerous books and scholarly articles. He is editor of *California Management Review* and has numerous professorships to his credit, including affiliate professor at the Goldman School of Public Policy and the Haas School of Business.

Lorin Woolfe has organized and delivered for Manufacturers Hanover Trust, E. F. Hutton, Deloitte, the Institute of Management Accountants, and others. He also served as a specialist in leadership at the American Management Association and vice president of program development for Drake, Beam, Morin (DBM), a globally recognized career management firm. As a student of the Bible and religion most of his life, he combined his studies with his professional experiences and is the author of *The Bible on Leadership*.

Gary Yukl holds a PhD from the University of California at Berkeley and is a professor at the State University of New York at Albany. He is the author of the text *Leadership in Organizations*, which focuses on effective leadership in organizations through both theory and practice. His book combines theory and his research on leadership, providing an insightful look at the use of power and how its components can influence the behavior of subordinates and peers.

Chapter 4

Interpersonal Leadership

▪▪The most important single ingredient in the formula of success is knowing how to get along with people.**▪▪**

—Theodore Roosevelt

Introduction

The importance for EMS leaders to develop strong interpersonal skills cannot be overemphasized. EMS leaders will be required to interact with subordinates, peers, and superiors every day under a variety of circumstances and conditions. According to David Nelson, a motivational speaker who holds a doctorate in ministry and whose work focuses on appreciative inquiry and supervision, found that according to "recent research conducted by the Gallop Institute the single most important factor in job performance and satisfaction is the relationship an employee has with his or her direct supervisor." The interaction with others does not stop in the workplace for the EMS leader. EMS leaders also have to deal with the public and representatives of other agencies before, during, and after emergency calls, as well as field and respond to their concerns and complaints. Unfortunately, as Ferris, Davidson, & Perrewe (2005) wrote in an article on developing political skill at work for *Training* magazine, "most of today's formal education conveys content-related knowledge while ignoring the skills of human interaction and effective influence." Despite this educational handicap with respect to interpersonal skills, how we interact and connect with others greatly affects our day-to-day and long-term success as an EMS leader.

The Effect of Listening on Interpersonal Connection

For a leader, a key element of the interpersonal connection is listening to what others have to say. Think about a time when you attempted to speak with someone about something important and

▪▪If you can't listen, you can't lead.**▪▪**

–George H. W. Bush, 41st President of the United States

that person did not look up from his desk, or she answered her cell phone, or he looked at an e-mail. Did you feel like you were important to them, or that you were bothering them? Now, as an EMS leader, think about whether you may have done the very same thing to someone else. Being distracted when someone is trying to discuss something that is important to them leaves the perception that you aren't listening and don't care. Taking the time to put down the cell phone, close that book, or turn away from the computer and focus your attention on someone will go a long way toward showing others that their need to discuss something with you is important.

The simple act of listening quietly and attentively until the other person has finished speaking will go a long way toward improving communication and strengthening relationships. All too often we finish each other's sentences, prepare our response before the other person is done speaking, and multitask while listening. Each of these mistakes takes away from communication and may even drive a wedge between the people attempting to communicate. Taking the time to listen, to give useful feedback, and to react appropriately to someone's concerns, not just their words or how they deliver them, will serve the EMS leader well.

Empathy

Empathy is a people skill that allows us to appreciate ourselves and the people around us. The better we understand ourselves and the unique experiences we bring to an organization, the easier it will be for us to accept and understand that the people around us also bring unique experiences, values, and perspectives. Empathy is about making a connection. Sympathy is feeling for someone, but empathy is feeling with someone, because you understand. Empathy practiced with sincerity and that is genuine, not superficial, is a shared connection that lets people know that their concerns and problems matter. According to John Gray, author of *Mars and Venus in the Workplace: A Practical Guide for Improving Communication and Getting Results at Work* and best known for his work in the fields of communication and relationships, "when employees are more emotionally fulfilled they are naturally more motivated, creative, productive, and cooperative." Therefore, by taking care of your people you will enable them to take care of themselves. The result is happier people who will do more for themselves, their leaders, and their organization.

Etiquette

Etiquette is centered in respect—for yourself and your patients, coworkers, friends, and family. EMS providers who have ever been relieved from duty late or left with a dirty or unstocked vehicle or station have experienced firsthand the impact of poor professional etiquette manifested in others' lack of respect. EMS leaders must hold themselves to a higher standard. They need to set the example by being on time or early for work, projecting a professional image with a clean uniform or suit, and returning phone calls and e-mails in a timely manner. Perhaps Barbara Pachter, who has consulted for such organizations as NASA and Motorola on the topic of communications, provides the best insight on this topic in her book *The Power of Positive Confrontation* (Pachter & Magee, 2000). She writes,

Stages of the Listening Process

- Hearing
- Focusing on the message
- Comprehending and interpreting
- Analyzing and evaluating
- Responding
- Remembering

Source: Interpersonal Skills for Leadership (Fritz, Brown, Lunde, & Banset, 2005).

"*Too many managers don't listen because they think they have all the answers or simply lack the patience to listen.***"**

–Steve Adubato, author of *Make the Connection: Improve Your Communication at Home and at Work.*

6 Keys to Active Listening

- Eliminate distractions
- Expect moments of silence and be comfortable with appropriate silence
- Concentrate on making good eye contact
- Clear your mind and focus on hearing what the speaker is saying
- Avoid snap judgments
- If you take notes, put your pen down when not writing to refocus on listening

Source: 6 Habits of Highly Effective Bosses (Kohn, 2005).

> **"Empathy focuses on communicating with others in a way that makes them feel uniquely understood."**
>
> –Stephen E. Kohn, coauthor of *6 Habits of Highly Effective Bosses*

> **"Professional etiquette is more than just making nice. It's how you show your respect for people."**
>
> –Thom Dick, author of *People Care*

"Etiquette is all about treating others the right way. The right way means with tact in both your words and actions. It's what you say and how you say it. It's treating people with kindness." Etiquette comes down to this— respect. It requires respect for yourself, the public, your people, your superiors, and your organization.

Perception

Dan Limmer and Mike O'Keefe have perhaps 50 years of experience in EMS between them, both career and volunteer. When we think back to EMT training, we are reminded that part of an EMS provider's patient assessment is forming a "general impression" that, according to Limmer and O'Keefe in their EMT text *Emergency Care*, "is based on the patient's chief complaint and appearance." In essence, this is our clinical application of the use of perception to form opinions as to the nature and severity of illness or injury. However, the perception we gain from our general impression, although important, is just part of the puzzle. We still must complete the rest of our assessment to better render care appropriate to the patient and his or her circumstances.

In the clinical setting, we can make decisions such as requesting additional resources based on our general impression. For EMS leaders, our perception of something we observe or that is reported to us is often just the tip of the iceberg. Although as leaders we can make some decisions based on our perception of a situation, such as whether the situation must be addressed immediately, making final decisions based solely on our perception of a situation or an individual is short-sighted and has great potential for negative consequences. So, just as general impression is only a component of the field provider's assessment, so too should perception be only a part of the leader's assessment.

Language of Leadership

- **Empathy**–Projection of one's own personality into the personality of another to understand him or her better; ability to share in another's emotions or feelings
- **Etiquette**–Forms, manners, and ceremonies established by convention as acceptable or required in social relations, in a profession, or in official life
- **General Impression**–Impression of the patient's condition that is formed on first approaching the patient, based on the patient's environment, chief complaint, and appearance
- **Perception**–Mental grasp of objects, qualities, etc., by means of the senses

Values

One's values are their beliefs as they relate to such things as honesty, fairness, compassion, and loyalty. Choosing to act consistently in keeping with our values is the challenge we all face on a daily basis. We aren't born with values. They develop over time from our experiences and we learn them from our families, friends, classmates, coworkers, bosses, what we see on the news, and any number of other sources. As children, we begin to accept values when we place importance on things we enjoy. As we grow from childhood to adolescence, we begin to express our preference for things and to actively choose from alternatives. Moving from adolescence to adulthood, we develop our commitment to the values we have chosen and become increasingly willing to take a stand on our values. For EMS leaders, it is important to understand what values are and how differences in values between personnel can affect cohesiveness and can challenge them in performance of their duties. Be aware, too, that there may be differences in values between an EMS leader and his or her personnel, and even among EMS leaders.

Vision

For a leader in any field or endeavor, having a vision for oneself and one's organization lays a foundation for the future, but simply having a vision is only the beginning—you must be able to

Leadership Through the Hollywood Lens

The television series "MASH" spanned 11 seasons. At the beginning of the fourth season, Colonel Sherman T. Potter (played by Harry Morgan) replaces interim commanding officer Major Frank Burns (Larry Linville). When company clerk Radar O'Reilly (Gary Burghoff) receives the official orders for the change of command, he is reluctant to pass the word to Major Burns for fear of his reaction. He seeks out the guidance and support of his long-time mentor and friend Captain Hawkeye Pierce (Alan Alda). Pierce and Captain BJ Hunnicut (Mike Farrell) have concerns about the new commanding officer that go beyond Frank's likely reaction, because Potter is a career Army officer who has not been in surgery for 2 years. Knowing that the personnel of the 4077th MASH unit work well together but do not take to strong military discipline is at the heart of their organizational concerns, and Potter's time away from surgery compounds Pierce's concerns about his ability to adequately contribute in surgery.

When Colonel Potter arrives, his demeanor and appearance of stern leadership reinforce the perception that the medically talented but militarily loose personnel of the 4077th are in for some abrupt changes in their way of life. When the first batch of casualties after Potter's arrival is received, Pierce and Hunnicut, along with head nurse Major Margaret Houlihan (Loretta Swit), discuss how they are going to monitor their new commanding officer's surgical skills. The colonel's performance in surgery begins to allay their concerns, and afterward the three doctors have an opportunity to unwind and get to know one another on a more personal level. From that point forward in the episode and the series, Colonel Potter is seen in a different light. Their time together had revealed that initial perceptions are only part of the picture and are not reflective of reality.

Back in the real world in which we live and work, I am certain that each of us can think of instances in which we either perceived someone or were ourselves perceived as something different from reality. Sometimes perception is right on the money and other times it misses the mark. Perhaps we as EMS leaders can draw on an existing skill used in patient care, the ongoing assessment, and apply it to our daily activities and interactions outside the patient care realm.

articulate it to the people who will help you see it through, and together you must map out how to achieve the vision. Fritz et al. (2005) lay out a three-step approach that begins with creating a vision statement, follows up with goal statements, and concludes with committing the energy to the strategic action steps. The vision statement lights the fire and sets the direction; it is the all-important "big picture." Goal statements should be realistic and achievable and will keep you and your people on track. For the final step, maintaining a commitment of energy will require that the goals remain visible so that you and your people remain motivated. Use the goal statements as a form of progress report as you move toward your goal—much like the organizations that post giant thermometers on their lawns during fundraisers to show their progress in reaching their goals.

Trust

In 1996, Francis Fukuyama wrote that "the decline of trust in the United States is evident in any number of changes in American society" (as cited in Fritz et al., 2005). His observations included such things as increased violence, litigation, and even the breakdown of social structures such as neighborhoods and organizations. This is important to us as EMS leaders because the trust the public places in our organizations and our people to care for them in their darkest hour is a sacred obligation we must live up to. As EMS leaders, we must maintain trust with both our people and the public. If we establish and nurture an atmosphere of honesty and integrity within our organization, trust is unlikely to become an issue. In his book *People Care*, Thom Dick (2005) wrote, "probably not much in medicine is sillier than an 18-year-old kid getting out of high school, then graduating from an EMT class with a 120-hour certificate and being expected to act like a professional." We need to be able to trust that our people will do the right thing and provide them not only with the equipment to do their job safely and effectively but also with the moral and ethical guidance to do it with honor and to treat everyone with dignity.

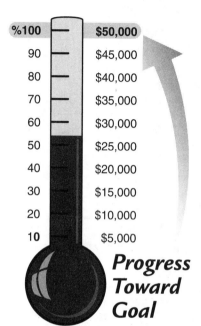

An example of a fundraising progress billboard.

Diversity

In the modern workplace, just as in modern society, diversity is a part of everyday life. Some of the more common aspects of diversity include culture, religion, and gender. As EMS providers, we encounter many of these differences, some subtle and some more obvious, in our practice of emergency care with patients, their families, and our coworkers and the other professionals with whom we come in contact. Therefore, in our role as EMS leaders, we must be more acutely aware of the nuances than we were as providers and must be prepared not only to set the standard of fairness and equality but also to step in when we witness comments or actions that may not be sensitive to the environment of diversity.

Leadership Lessons from History

Unlike Washington, Jefferson, and Lincoln, who held public offices of power and authority, Martin Luther King Jr. provided his leadership and vision as a citizen and minister. In the 1950s and 1960s he led a nonviolent protest movement designed to raise awareness and make the equality of man envisioned in the Declaration of Independence a reality. From the steps of the Lincoln Memorial on August 28, 1963, he delivered his now famous "I Have a Dream" speech, which is credited as a catalyst to the movement that led to the enactment of the Civil Rights Act of 1964. In recognition of the impact of his vision and his ability to lead and organize others in support of it, he was later awarded the Nobel Peace Prize.

Key Elements of a Climate of Trust

1. Sharing and listening to personal events and concerns
2. Vulnerability and acceptance of human error
3. Loyalty to the organization and its goals and leaders
4. Accepting others and welcoming their unique behaviors
5. Involving others in decision making
6. Valuing the ideas of others
7. Awareness and sensitivity to the needs of others
8. Clear oral and written communication
9. Openness and willingness to explore new experiences
10. Honesty and the avoidance of deceit

Source: A Handbook of Structured Experiences for Human Relations Training (Pfeiffer & Jones, 1981).

Language of Leadership

- **Values**—The social principles, goals, or standards held or accepted by an individual, class, or society
- **Vision**—The ability to perceive something as through mental acuteness or keen foresight
- **Trust**—A firm belief or confidence in the honesty, integrity, reliability, and justice of another person or thing

"Without a positive understanding of how we are different, it is easy to misinterpret and incorrectly assess each other.**"**

–John Gray, author of *Mars and Venus in the Workplace: A Practical Guide for Improving Communication and Getting Results at Work*

Conflict Resolution

When people and groups are interdependent, the likelihood of human conflict increases and, some might argue, is inevitable. According to Suzette Haden Elgin, PhD, founder of the Ozark Center for Language Studies, "most adults in our society have a knee-jerk negative reaction to commands and criticism—to being told what to do." This is important for EMS leaders to understand because our profession at times demands that orders be given and followed without question (such as at emergency scenes) and that constructive criticism, such as in the Quality Assurance and Improvement Process, be provided to our staff. Understanding that there is a normal process of development in any conflict, how it manifests itself, and some strategies for addressing the conflict will improve our ability to resolve conflict.

The Conflict Development Cycle

Stage	Individual Thought or Action
Frustration	I am blocked from satisfying a goal or concern.
Conceptualization	I begin to determine what the problem is. I begin to attribute motives and blame based on my perceptions.
Behavior	I act on the perceptions above. (There is a cycle of reinforcement between conceptualization and behavior. How I act is determined by what I believe about the other party. How I act determines how the other perceives my motives and how he or she consequently acts.)
Outcome	The conflict is resolved in one of three ways: win–lose, lose–lose, or win–win, depending on the behavior of both parties.

Source: Interpersonal Skills for Leadership (Fritz et al., 2005).

Conflict often results from a misunderstanding based on perception and assumptions about what took place as well as the attitudes and motives behind the behavior. Although conflict is viewed as negative or bad by many, the reality is that conflict is perhaps inevitable in the human experience. Therefore, while conflict may on the surface be negative, how we as leaders approach it could reap benefits. In fact, according to Fritz et al. (2005), "constructive conflict is functional because it helps members accomplish goals and generate new insights into old problems." Knowing that conflict can and will occur and that how we respond to it could substantially change the outcome, we as EMS leaders must develop a positive and proactive versus a negative and reactionary approach to handling conflict in our organizations.

> **"**The challenge for EMS managers when conflict occurs is not to avoid it, but to look for the opportunities that come along with conflict.**"**
>
> –Gary Ludwig, Deputy Fire Chief, Memphis (Tennessee) Fire Department

When a conflict develops that must be resolved, it is important to approach it in a way and at an appropriate time that minimize the fallout from both the initial conflict and the resolution process. Whether or not the conflict may result in disciplinary action, it is important not to allow emotions to dictate your behavior or response to the matter. "Emotions can cloud your judgment and prevent an objective assessment" (Ludwig, 2004). It is also important to remember that resolving a dispute will not alter the underlying conflict of interest that generated the dispute. J. Thomas Wren, who teaches at the University of Richmond's Jepson School of Leadership Studies, reminds us that, "[a]s long as the relationship endures future disputes will arise." Therefore, when addressing conflict, it is important not only to resolve the immediate concerns of the people involved but also to address the root cause so that the likelihood of similar future occurrences will be minimized.

The Power of the "Thank You"

When it comes to interpersonal connection, perhaps the simplest gesture for building rapport is to show your appreciation for another person's efforts. Whether by just saying "thank you" to a member of your team for being consistently on time or jotting a quick thank you note in recognition of extra effort, showing people that what they do is important to you not only will build trust but will reinforce good behavior and motivate others to continue to perform well. If your people hear from you only when they do something incorrectly, their perception will be that the only way to get your attention is to make a mistake or do something wrong. As children we are taught how and when to say please and thank you, but often as adults we lose sight of how important these simple gestures are. Take a moment to think about how good it felt the last time someone said thank you for something you did. Now think back to the last time you thanked someone for the work that he or she did versus the last time you spoke to an employee about something that was done wrong. If your last encounter with one of your people was negative, make the next few encounters positive ones. If your last few encounters with your people were positive, keep up the good work—you are right on track.

You Are the EMS Leader

It is approaching 7 am and the heart of the morning shift change. As you go about your duties of facilitating offgoing and oncoming units, you overhear one of your field personnel raising her voice on her cell phone. Her behavior is somewhat disruptive to the rest of the personnel in the room. As you approach her, you realize that she appears to be arguing with a dispatcher about having just been dispatched on a call although there are only minutes until the end of her shift.

1. *What are your immediate concerns about the overall situation?*

2. *Would you initially approach the situation differently if the call had been reassigned to another unit than you would if it was still assigned to her unit? Why or why not? What, if any differences would there be to your approach?*

Later in the day, after the initial issues were addressed, you begin to contemplate how you will follow up with this employee and the dispatcher. You spend some time speaking with other supervisors and find out that this employee and the dispatcher have had words in the past, with each other and with others. Additionally, you discover that her unit was dispatched so close to shift change in part because of the tardiness of personnel on the unit that was to relieve her.

3. *How do these additional factors affect your approach to following up with this matter?*

4. *At what point and in what way will you approach the individuals involved? Will you include speaking with the personnel who were late as part of the process or address this as a separate issue?*

5. *Does the late-relief issue excuse or perhaps mitigate the behavior of the provider who was yelling at the dispatcher? Why or why not?*

Chapter Summary

The relationships we as EMS leaders develop with our subordinates, peers, and superiors will have a significant effect on our effectiveness as leaders. Listening to concerns and understanding that perhaps our initial perceptions may tell only part of the story are important concepts for leaders in EMS to understand and practice. Leaders must have strong values and must not allow emotions to dictate behavior. To implement vision, leaders must be organized and build trust and respect with the people around them. Setting the standard of respect for everyone's diverse backgrounds and views allows EMS leaders to build their moral and earned authority, which will translate into greater short-term and long-term success. Having this solid foundation in place will allow the leader to both minimize the frequency of conflict and address conflict effectively when it inevitably arises. In EMS, everything we do is ultimately about people, and thus solid people skills are a necessity for the EMS leader.

Why Their Views Matter: About the Individuals Cited in the Chapter

Steve Adubato is a four-time Emmy Award–winning television anchor on Thirteen/WNET New York (PBS). He has appeared as a media and communication expert on FOX News, MSNBC, and CNN. He has also distinguished himself as a columnist with the *Newark Star Ledger*, as a motivational speaker, and as author of a number of books, including *Make the Connection: Improve Your Communication at Home and at Work* and *Speak from the Heart: Be Yourself and Get Results*.

Elizabeth A. Banset is an instructional consultant and coauthor of the text *Interpersonal Skills for Leadership*.

F. William Brown is an associate professor at the College of Business at Montana State University, Bozeman. He is coauthor of the text *Interpersonal Skills for Leadership*.

George H. W. Bush became the 41st president of the United States after serving as Ronald Reagan's vice president for 8 years. He was a lieutenant junior grade in the U.S. Navy and flew 58 missions as a pilot during World War II. He spent 4 years in the House of Representatives, was ambassador to the United Nations, and served as director of the Central Intelligence Agency. His presidency was defined in large part by his core values of honor and decency and a commitment to do the right thing.

Sherry L. Davidson is a professor of education at New York University and coauthor of *Political Skill at Work: Impact on Work Effectiveness*.

Thom Dick has been a passionate advocate of EMS patients and their caregivers for more than 35 years. He spent more than 23 years as an EMT and paramedic in San Diego County. He is the author of a number of monthly columns in several EMS journals. He is a well-known international speaker and the coauthor of the book *People Care: Career Friendly Practices for Professional Caregivers*.

Suzette Haden Elgin is the founder of the Ozark Center for Language Studies and Associate Professor Emerita of Linguistics at San Diego State University. She has written a dozen books, many of which discuss a variety of topics relating to communications, and she is well known as a seminar leader and public speaker.

Gerald R. Ferris is the Francis Eppes Professor of Management and Professor of Psychology at Florida State University. He received his PhD in business administration from the University of Illinois at Urbana–Champaign. His research interests are in the areas of interpersonal and political influence in organizations, performance evaluation, and strategic human resources management. He has written more than 100 articles for a variety of scholarly journals. He has consulted for such companies as ARCO, Eli Lilly, and Motorola.

Susan Fritz is an associate professor in the Department of Agricultural Leadership, Education, and Communication at the University of Nebraska at Lincoln. She is coauthor of the text *Interpersonal Skills for Leadership*.

Francis Fukuyama earned his BA degree from Cornell University and his PhD from Harvard University. He is the author of a number of books and articles and is a professor of international political economy and the director of the International Development Program at the Paul H. Nitze School of Advanced International Studies at Johns Hopkins University.

John Gray is an internationally recognized expert in the fields of communication and relationships. He has written more than a dozen books, including *Mars and Venus in the Workplace: A Practical Guide for Improving Communication and Getting Results at Work*, and has been conducting personal growth seminars for more than 30 years.

Stephen E. Kohn is a licensed mental health professional who is highly respected and experienced as an executive coach. Before starting his own firm, Work & People Solutions, he served as executive vice president for Paul Sherman & Associates. As a graduate of Cornell University and Adelphi University's Graduate School, his education and his experience provide solid credentials. One of his areas of expertise is motivating leaders to develop methods to maximize the potential of people who report to them. He is coauthor of the book *6 Habits of Highly Effective Bosses*.

Dan Limmer is a passionate educator and the coauthor of *Emergency Care*. He has been involved in EMS for more than 25 years and is a paramedic with the Kennebunk Fire Rescue and Kennebunkport EMS in Maine. Dan teaches EMT and paramedic courses at Southern Maine Technical College. He is a charter member of the National Association of EMS Educators and speaks regularly at state, regional, and national EMS conferences.

Gary Ludwig is Deputy Fire Chief of the Memphis (Tennessee) Fire Department. He has more than 30 years of experience in fire and EMS, including 25 years with the City of St. Louis, from which he retired at the rank of chief paramedic. He also served as president of the IAFC EMS Section. He regularly writes on the topic of leadership for national trade magazines and shares his insights at conferences throughout the United States.

Joyce Povlacs Lunde is Professor Emeritus, Department of Agricultural Leadership, Education, and Communication at the University of Nebraska at Lincoln. She is coauthor of the text *Interpersonal Skills for Leadership*.

Susan Magee is coauthor of *The Power of Positive Confrontation* and an award-winning writer whose articles and stories have appeared in many magazines and newspapers across the country.

David E. Nelson received his Doctor of Ministry from the Lutheran School of Theology. He is a personal empowerment coach, motivational speaker, consultant, and trainer with an emphasis and passion for the area of appreciative inquiry. Among his many speaking engagements, he discussed appreciative supervision at the Navigator emergency communications conference in Baltimore, Maryland, in 2007.

Michael F. O'Keefe became the Vermont EMS State Training Coordinator in 1989 and was chosen to participate in the development of the U.S. Department of Transportation National Standard EMS Curricula. He is coauthor of *Emergency Care* and *Essentials of Emergency Care* and a contributing writer for *Paramedic Care: Principles and Practice*. Mike remains active as a volunteer EMS provider and speaks often at a variety of conferences.

Barbara Pachter is a business communications consultant, speaker, and seminar leader. Her clients have included NASA, Merck, and IBM. She is an adjunct professor at Rutgers University and the author of multiple books, including *When Little Things Count...And They Always Do* and *The Power of Positive Confrontation*, which she coauthored with Susan Magee.

Pamela L. Perrewe is a Distinguished Research Professor and the Haywood and Betty Taylor Eminent Scholar at the College of Business, Department of Management, at Florida State University, where she is the director of the Human Resource Management Center. She holds an MS degree and PhD in business administration from the University of Nebraska at Lincoln. She is a widely published author of research and other articles, book chapters, and books.

Theodore Roosevelt was the 26th president of the United States, assuming the presidency in 1901 when William McKinley was assassinated. Roosevelt previously had been a colonel in the U.S. Army and a state assemblyman and governor of New York. Although he was known for his aggressive style, he was a deft and subtle diplomat.

J. Thomas Wren teaches at the University of Richmond's Jepson School of Leadership Studies. He is the author of *The Leader's Companion: Insights on Leadership Through the Ages*.

Chapter 5

Leadership Communication

❝Real communication happens when people feel safe.**❞**

—Ken Blanchard

Introduction

During training, emergency medical technicians (EMTs) and paramedics study communications with an emphasis on the radio and telephone in relation to operational issues, such as being dispatched to a call, communicating with other units, and making contact with a medical control physician. In the core curriculum, there is little if any real focus on communicating with each other or even with patients and their families. Although there are scenarios throughout the curriculum that provide examples, there is no real focus on the nuances of communications with other people.

As an aspiring, new, or even experienced EMS leader, understanding the positive and negative impacts of effective communication with others is essential. Developing and improving one's communication skills are also important. In EMS, there is so much more to communications than speaking clearly on the radio, asking the patient about his or her medical history, and filling out a patient care report. Perhaps the biggest misconception about communication is the belief that what was said is what was heard. Often the communicator's intent, tone, circumstances, and motives make a difference in how the intended message is received and understood. To be most effective, leaders in EMS must understand the importance of communication in order to develop their vision and achieve their desires.

Persuasion

Leaders, and followers as well, use communication to persuade and influence others. A child in a store tries to convince mom that he needs a certain toy, a politician campaigns for his constituents'

> **❝**Ineffective communication is a lot more common than effective communication.**❞**
>
> –Steve Adubato, Four-Time Emmy Award-Winning Television Anchor

votes, and a supervisor explains a new policy to her staff. Throughout history, human beings have worked to persuade others to support their ideas and desires. Roger Soder, author of *The Language of Leadership*, reminds us that "persuasion is important both in itself and as a function of leadership," and "the importance of persuasion and the subtlety with which persuasion must at times be effected" cannot be overstated. Having this understanding as well as an ability to communicate in a way that encourages others to follow is a critical component of leadership.

From a leadership perspective, persuasion and communication are inextricably connected. The old-school "do as I say, not as I do" approach to leadership is not acceptable and is ineffective. Often in EMS, if the leader has not walked a mile in the follower's shoes during his or her career, the leader is seen differently than someone who rose up through the ranks and, in the eyes of the follower, "paid their dues."

There are three distinct modes of persuasion that will further our understanding of its impact on leadership: ethos, pathos, and logos. Each has its distinctions, and leaders must understand not only how to use them effectively but also how to respond appropriately to their use by others. It is important that the EMS leader understand that the message is only part of the story. Ensuring that the message is presented in a manner that is most appropriate to the situation and the people involved will go a long way toward achieving the desired results.

For ethos, the speaker's character plays a chief role in persuasion and aids the audience in finding the speaker credible, thus giving validity to the speaker's cause. When implementing pathos, the speaker must evoke an emotional response in the audience that helps to align them with the speaker's sympathies. Finally, logos employs reason through the use of a logical and methodical argument presented with the speaker's actual words.

Language of Leadership

Leaders persuade followers with these communication tools:

- **Ethos**
  - The distinguishing character, sentiment, moral nature, or guiding beliefs of a person, group, or institution
  - How believable or trustworthy the leader is
- **Pathos**
  - An element in experience or in artistic representation evoking pity or compassion
  - How the leader reaches out to the emotions of the audience
- **Logos**
  - Speech, word, reason. In ancient Greek philosophy, reason is the controlling principle in the universe
  - How the speech itself explains and persuades through words and logic

"It can be argued that the reputation of the character preceding a speaker is of considerable importance."

–Roger Soder, author of *The Language of Leadership*

Nonverbal Communication

Nonverbal communication includes appearance, body language, eye contact, facial expressions, and proxemics. In fact, "[v]arious experts in communication estimate that between 75% and 90% of the information we gather from others is nonverbal in nature" (Fritz et al., 2005). In the field, EMS providers read nonverbal signs of fear, anxiety, anger, and sometimes joy in the faces of patients and their families. On the flip side, patients and their families learn about their provider through the EMT's appearance, grooming, and approach. These attributes can create a sense of professionalism and indicate the provider's level of concern.

For EMS providers, assessment of a patient includes a general impression that we develop within the first moments of contact. Appearance is a two-way street. Arriving for work on time, in a clean uniform and neatly groomed, sends a message of professionalism and shows a desire to meet responsibilities. In contrast, someone who shows up in a dirty or wrinkled uniform sends a far less appealing message to his or her coworkers and to the public.

Leadership Lessons from History

Ethos is the effect that a person's character or reputation has on his or her ability to persuade others. If, for example, a leader's ethics or reputation is tarnished, it will be difficult for him or her to communicate a message effectively, whereas a leader with a strong reputation for fairness will have an easier time. In the post-Watergate world, it may be difficult to think of Richard M. Nixon as having character. However, in the book *Nixon's Ten Commandments of Statecraft*, author James C. Humes discusses Nixon's tendency to edit speeches for substance, as compared to, for example, Reagan's inclination to edit for style. Humes writes of Nixon that "he had contempt for those politicians who would read the speeches prepared for them for the first time before they descended to make their talk in the ballroom." According to Humes, Nixon liked to draft his speeches on a yellow pad or at least to enumerate to the speechwriters the key points he wanted to cover. Humes also quotes a conversation he had with Nixon in which Nixon said, "Principles are not picked out like Calvin Klein ties that can be discarded when they are out of fashion." In my view, Humes believes Nixon to be genuine and not "packaged" by his handlers. To Humes, it appears that Nixon was about substance, not style, and that his substance was his character. Ultimately, Nixon may have chosen to resign in part because he realized that his actions had damaged his character to the point where he could no longer effectively communicate as a leader.

Logos is persuasion based on logic or reason, essentially a "just the facts" approach. There will be times when a more concrete or logical approach is warranted for sending a message. In these instances, appealing to another's logical side might work best. In considering logic as a tool of persuasion, President Woodrow Wilson's Fourteen-Points speech of 1918 is a clear embodiment of the use of logic at the core of a persuasive argument. In his speech, Wilson makes many absolute statements, such as "the only secrecy of counsel, the only lack of fearless frankness, the only failure to make definite statement of the objects of the war, lies with Germany and her allies" and "all the peoples of the world are in effect partners in this interest, and for our own part we see very clearly that unless justice be done to others it will not be done to us." Clearly, Wilson was a man of conviction in his beliefs and used what he considered to be logical and orderly absolutes as the basis of his argument.

Pathos is an appeal to one's emotions. In some situations, appealing to the emotions of an audience might be the best approach. President Ronald Reagan had a successful career as an actor before seeking public office. He used the acting skills he developed through his many film roles to persuade others to visualize his perspective. Reagan became known as the Great Communicator "because of his skill at talking evocatively and using folksy anecdotes that ordinary people could understand" (Cannon, 2004). In his inaugural address, Reagan used his charm and powers of persuasion to help us believe such words as "government can and must provide opportunity, not smother it; foster productivity, not stifle it." He appealed to our emotions and our desire to be better off tomorrow. Reagan appealed to people because he had a natural connection with them. He paid attention to the reactions to his speeches and used optimism effectively as a leadership tool. As a result of their belief in him and in his words, people also began to believe in themselves.

When communicating, hand gestures, eye contact, and body language become part of the message. Therefore, it is important that these are all consistent with each other because any apparent contradiction between words and attitudes will suggest insincerity to the listener. If you are perceived to be disingenuous, a clear message as well as any previously developed trust will be undermined.

Yet another consideration in communicating with others is the impact of physical space. The study of informal space is known as proxemics, and its lessons can be valuable to both EMS leaders and providers. Although there are variations from one culture to the next, in American society there are general norms regarding intimate, personal, and social space. Culture need not mean ethnicity or race; for example, in some sports cultures, it is an acceptable and encouraging gesture to give a slap on the buttocks. Clearly, this is not something that would be acceptable in many other workplaces, including EMS. The reality is that something as simple as a misunderstood look or touch can become a nightmare for anyone in a leadership capacity. Taking the time to build a reputation of fairness and clear communication is the best course of action. It is important for EMS leaders to understand this concept so that an otherwise innocuous interaction is not misunderstood by a subordinate, peer, or superior.

For EMS leaders, it is of the utmost importance that the effect of nonverbal communication on the effectiveness of one's connections with others is understood. Taking the skills honed as a provider through patient encounters and putting these to use in a leadership role will enhance your ability to provide leadership to your people.

Language of Leadership

The following is a general outline of the standards that apply in American culture:

- **Intimate Space**—Generally up to 18 inches; reserved for interactions with family and close friends
- **Personal Space**—Where most interpersonal interactions take place; generally ranges from approximately 18 inches to about 4 feet
- **Social Space**—The area in which more formal interactions take place; ranges from 4 to 12 feet
- **Public Space**—The area in which things like large audience interactions take place; generally more than 12 feet

Source: Interpersonal Skills for Leadership (Fritz et al., 2005).

Peer Pressure

The topic of communications also includes the effect of peer pressure on the actions of personnel in EMS. Since peer pressure can be effective, it is appropriate to discuss its potential effects as a continuation of our discussion of persuasion. Often, policy may say one thing, but a more senior EMT or paramedic may persuade a newer provider that overlooking a particular policy is okay. Through their influence, they would thus be establishing a norm in the field that may not be acceptable to the organization or its leadership. The problem arises when the more junior person is caught violating or ignoring the policy and must then pay the consequences. Will he or she tell you that the senior paramedic said this behavior is permitted? Most likely, the junior person will not, for fear of not being accepted by his or her peers. Are the peers who said the violation was acceptable going to step forward and take the hit? Not likely. How then do we as EMS leaders address such situations involving the negative use of peer influence? The importance of remaining accessible to and approachable by our subordinates cannot be overemphasized. Additionally, and perhaps most importantly, we must develop the ability to listen to our people and value their input.

Accessibility and Approachability

We often hear of the "open-door" policy many managers have. However, accessibility is just part of the equation. Leaders must also be approachable, that is, they must create a comfortable environment for personnel so that they do not feel apprehensive about voicing a concern. To quote an esteemed colleague who is an EMS provider and educator, "people don't care how much you know until they know how much you care" (cited by Crouchman, 2005). When people sense that you care, that you will listen, and that you will attempt to help them with their concerns, they will be more inclined to share them with you.

Listening

Active listening is essential to success as both an EMS provider and a leader. However, in their book *Interpersonal Skills for Leadership*, Fritz et al. remind us of the reality that "very little time (if any) is devoted to teaching people the skills they need to become better listeners." For an EMT or a paramedic, the ability to pick up on the nuances of what patients and their families say during an assessment contributes greatly to providing better care. This means better care for their injuries, illness, or even simply filling their basic human need for someone to listen. In the role of EMS leader, you can apply that same skill of active listening to encounters with peers, subordinates, and even superiors to improve your ability to meet their needs.

Listening can be passive or it can be active. It is important for leaders to understand the difference and to develop both active and passive listening skills. It is important to understand that hearing and listening are not synonymous and that, as Kate Boyd Dernocoeur writes in her book *Streetsense: Communication, Safety, and Control*, "without listening you can hear what people say and yet miss the meaning of their words." Developing active listening skills will make you a more effective leader because you will absorb more of the meaning from the words you hear. According to Steve Adubato, who has appeared as a media and communication expert on FOX News, MSNBC, and CNN, "when your people come to realize that you are not listening to them, they begin to shut down and stop making suggestions and being straight with you." In contrast, when the people around you sense that you are listening, they will believe that you care and that their opinions and feelings matter to you, even if you can't fix their problems.

> **"Listening is the most important element of communication."**
>
> –Tim Holman, author of *Leadership Rules of Engagement*

Written Communication

Written communication is as important, if not more important, than the spoken word in many organizations. Policies, memos, letters, incident reports, e-mails, and so many other forms of written communication are part of every organization and everyone's workday environment. Even those in positions where very little regular written communication takes place are guided in their work by documents created by their predecessors. An ability to communicate effectively and articulately through written media is an important skill for anyone who aspires to a leadership role.

During the last decade, e-mail has moved to the forefront of communication media, both formal and informal. Readily accessible in just about every home and office, e-mail is an intricate part of everyday life in modern society. Often it is simply a method for communication, but it can also be used to build an electronic paper trail and to track official documents. Additionally, while e-mail has become a fact of life and a common tool, just as with any other form of communication, it is important to understand when and how to use it. It is easy to quickly send an angry e-mail regarding a recent controversial event. In an article titled "Count to 10 Before You Discipline," Gary Ludwig, former chief paramedic with the city of St. Louis, advises that EMTs refrain from allowing emotions to dictate behavior when it comes to taking disciplinary action. Although

Leadership Through the Hollywood Lens

The Hollywood true story of *Erin Brockovich* is about a divorced mother of three whose tenacity lands her a job with a law firm that represents victims of corporate pollution. Played by Julia Roberts, Erin convinces her attorney, Ed Masry (Albert Finney), to hire her as an assistant in his law office. As she organizes his files, she notices comingled real estate and medical files that have a common link to a California power company. Erin finds this combination odd and asks Ed for permission to look into it further, and he approves. After a week of legwork outside the office, Erin returns to find that she has been fired because she didn't show up for work for a week. In her mind she was "working" the whole time on the power company case, while in the eyes of her boss and others in the office, she simply hadn't shown up for work. Clearly, Erin and Ed's interpretations of their earlier conversation regarding the case were quite different.

As the movie progresses, Erin meets and maintains contact with each of the victims who become part of a class action lawsuit. She is depicted as compassionate and a good listener who genuinely cares about the clients and their respective situations. When they begin to concentrate on the legal aspects of the case, Ed Masry brings in additional attorneys who are experts in the area of law but clearly lack the listening skills of Erin Brockovich. Many of the clients become upset and even angered at the change in approach and personnel. In the end, it is Erin's communications skills and trust she has earned through her ability to listen, coupled with her genuine concern, that leads her to success.

In both examples from this movie, we can see the importance of communications for both the leader and the follower. When Erin and Ed misunderstand one another early in the movie, Erin loses her job, and, later in the film, the case almost unravels due to poor communication between the lawyers and the clients. When Erin first speaks with the victims in the case, she has no earned authority with them, but through excellent listening, as well as by being accessible and approachable, Erin is able to build relationships and trust from the ground up.

As EMS providers, we have used our ability to listen and communicate with patients and their families to build trust rapidly with them as we take care of their immediate needs and concerns. Even when their needs may not be an emergency in our eyes, we listen and treat them with the same respect we would want to receive if the roles were reversed. As an EMS leader, listening to your people and making sure that your conversations are well understood by all involved parties will help to build trust and create a positive work environment. Be sure to take their concerns seriously, even when they may not appear to be a high priority.

his article focuses on controlling emotions specifically when establishing discipline, his message can easily be applied to the use of e-mail and other written messages sent by an unclear and agitated mind.

Written communication contains challenges not found in the spoken word. Written communication is more formal than when spoken, especially in a work environment. As a result of this formality, writers should usually avoid contractions, figures of speech, and conversational style. Accurate spelling is important to project intelligence and conscientiousness. Punctuation is important to the flow and readability of the written word. "Writing is hard, even for authors who do it all the time," writes Roger Angell in the foreword to William Strunk Jr., and E. B. White's *Elements of Style*. In the final analysis, writing requires more organization and forethought than does speaking, because a conversation develops as it goes and by nature is interactive.

Examining the written artifacts of your organization can help leaders and aspiring leaders to avoid the misuse of written media in the workplace. On the topic of written communications, Ronna Lichtenberg, coauthor of *Work Would Be Great if It Weren't for the People*, suggests that leaders "think of all the things people can do with your memos, all of the ways memos can be shared with those for whom they weren't intended, all the words that can be lifted out of context to hurt you." For example, an incident in my own organization began as a simple joke sent between coworkers, but resulted in disciplinary action for the sender, as well as great embarrassment for his superior—the subject of a humorous yet somewhat insulting e-mail. Although the message was intended only for a select group, the author unintentionally e-mailed the entire organization and ultimately damaged his superior's reputation. Considering Lichtenberg's cautionary words as well as my own personal experiences, I believe the message is clear: written communication should be well thought out and never sent in haste.

> **"***The greatest lessons I've learned about good leadership have been through my own mistakes and from bad examples.***"**
>
> —Hans Finzel, author of *The Ten Mistakes Leaders Make*

You Are the EMS Leader

On Thursday afternoon an employee comes to you during his shift and reports that he is not feeling well. You ensure that he is promptly seen by employee health. The employee returns with the appropriate forms signed by employee health and tells you that he is excused from work until Monday. You ask him if he has any shifts between now and then and he says no. As he prepares to leave, you ask if he needs anything and you offer get well wishes. He says he will be okay going home and thanks you for your concern. On Monday, you get a call that this same employee did not show up for his shift on Saturday, which created involuntary overtime, and you are asked to provide an explanation to the human resources manager. You explain the situation as described above and are instructed to issue a written reprimand to the employee for not informing you that he would be out sick for his Saturday shift.

1. *What are your thoughts and feelings on this situation and how would you proceed?*

2. *How would his past behavior affect your actions?*

3. *Although he did tell you that he had no shifts scheduled until after Monday, you did not double-check the schedule. Would this affect how you proceed? Why or why not?*

4. *Given your choice between taking responsibility for the miscommunication and not checking the schedule or allowing the blame to rest squarely on the shoulders of your subordinate, what impact could your decision in this case have on your earned authority and the perception of your ethos by your superiors and subordinates?*

Wrap-Up

Chapter Summary

In this chapter, we looked at the importance of effective communication. Through a historical analysis, we looked at how the use of ethos, pathos, and logos can be used by the leader to persuade people in the furtherance of their goals and objectives. With an emphasis on the leader's ability to connect with their people to build trust and create cooperation, we examined the importance of being both accessible and approachable as well as explored the development of active listening skills. Communication is a key element in all relationships, and for a leader, the ability to effectively communicate cohesively holds all other aspects of leadership together.

Why Their Views Matter: About the Individuals Cited in the Chapter

Steve Adubato is a four-time Emmy Award–winning television anchor on Thirteen/WNET New York (PBS). He has appeared as a media and communication expert on FOX News, MSNBC, and CNN. He has also distinguished himself as a columnist with the *Newark Star Ledger*, as a motivational speaker, and as author of a number of books, including *Make the Connection: Improve Your Communication at Home and at Work* and *Speak from the Heart: Be Yourself and Get Results*.

Roger Angell is nationally renowned for his work as a journalist for *The New Yorker Magazine* and, as the son of Katherine Sergeant White, a longtime editor at *The New Yorker*, and the stepson of E. B. White, coauthor of *The Elements of Style*, Angell has an extensive background in writing and editing. Known as "the poet laureate of baseball," he has been writing books and articles about the sport since 1962.

Ken Blanchard is the author of *Leadership and the One Minute Manager* as well as coauthor of *The One Minute Manager* and a number of other books on topics relating to leadership, management, and motivation. He has served as a consultant for a number of top corporations and is well known as a dynamic teacher and speaker. He is a polished storyteller with a knack for making the seemingly complex easy to understand. He received both his BA degree and his PhD from Cornell University, where he is a visiting lecturer and a trustee emeritus.

Elizabeth A. Banset is an instructional consultant and coauthor of the text *Interpersonal Skills for Leadership*.

F. William Brown is an associate professor at the College of Business at Montana State University, Bozeman. He is coauthor of the text *Interpersonal Skills for Leadership*.

Lou Cannon is a nonfiction author and biographer. Having written five books on the former president, he is considered by some to be the foremost biographer of Ronald Reagan.

Joseph Crouchman is a paramedic and bioterrorism educator with Liberty Health, Jersey City Medical Center Emergency Medical Services. He began his career in EMS in Texas in 1982. He has a passion for education and has been teaching for more than 17 years.

Kate Boyd Dernocoeur has been involved in EMS since 1973. Over the years she has lectured extensively in the United States and Canada. She worked as a paramedic in Denver City and Denver County. She is the author of *Streetsense: Communication, Safety, and Control* and coauthor of *Principles of Emergency Medical Dispatch*.

Hans Finzel is the author of *The Top Ten Mistakes Leaders Make* and at the time of its publication was executive director of a church planning and leadership training ministry operating in more than 60 countries. Previously he had served as a pastor in Long Beach, California, and spent a decade in Vienna, Austria. Dr. Finzel has authored several other books, including *Empowered Leaders*.

Susan Fritz is an associate professor in the Department of Agricultural Leadership, Education, and Communication at the University of Nebraska at Lincoln. She is coauthor of the text *Interpersonal Skills for Leadership*.

Tim Holman has an extensive background in healthcare management and the fire service. He served as chief of German Township Fire and EMS in Clark County, Ohio, and graduated with honors from Ottawa University in Kansas. Tim is a member of the National Speakers Association and is known for giving unique and motivating programs that provide practical solutions to attendees. He has written numerous articles for national journals and is the author of *Leadership Rules of Engagement: 25 Laws to Help Develop the Leader Within You*.

James C. Humes was a speechwriter for four American presidents. In addition to teaching at the University of Pennsylvania, he has written a number of books, including *Nixon's Ten Commandments of Statecraft*, *Confessions of a White House Ghostwriter*, and *The Wit and Wisdom of Churchill*.

Ronna Lichtenberg has appeared on CNN, NPR, and numerous television programs as a business expert. She is a contributing editor for *O, The Oprah Magazine*. She is president of Clear Peak Communications and a coauthor with Gene Stone of *Work Would Be Great If It Weren't for the People: Making Office Politics Work for You*.

Gary Ludwig is Deputy Fire Chief of the Memphis (Tennessee) Fire Department. He has more than 30 years of experience in fire and EMS, including 25 years with the City of St. Louis, from which he retired at the rank of chief paramedic. He also serves as president of the IAFC EMS Section. He regularly writes on the topic of leadership for national trade magazines and shares his insights at conferences throughout the United States.

Joyce Povlacs Lunde is Professor Emeritus, Department of Agricultural Leadership, Education, and Communication at the University of Nebraska at Lincoln. She is coauthor of the text *Interpersonal Skills for Leadership*.

Ronald Reagan was the 40th president of the United States. He served as a captain in the U.S. Army and was governor of California before being elected to the presidency in 1980. Reagan used his experience as an actor to hone his communications skills. He was known as the Great Communicator for his ability to present his ideas in an understandable way that was often illustrated with a joke or a story.

Roger Soder is a senior associate at the Center for Educational Renewal at the University of Washington. He is also vice president of the Institute for Educational Inquiry. In addition to authoring the book *The Language of Leadership*, he was the editor of the book *Democracy, Education, and the Schools*.

Woodrow Wilson was the 28th president of the United States. Previously, he had served as president of Princeton University and as governor of New Jersey. Before going into politics, he studied law and while in graduate school he published the book *Congressional Government*. Wilson believed in fusing power with principle and instituted regular White House press conferences and ended the practice of the president not addressing Congress in person.

Chapter 6

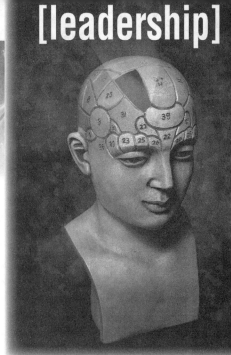

Understanding the Psychology of Leadership

> **"** Lead and inspire people. Don't try to manage and manipulate people. Inventories can be managed but people must be led. **"**

—Ross Perot

Introduction

Exploring the psychology of leadership in general and as it relates specifically to the EMS leader will enable a better understanding of our common human heritage and what motivates people to lead and to follow. Professor Howard Gardner of the Harvard Graduate School of Education states that "our understanding of the nature and processes of leadership is most likely to be enhanced as we come to understand better the arenas in which leadership necessarily occurs—namely, the human mind." Additionally, through a look at the unique psychological stresses faced in the world of EMS, we will better understand how such things as perspective, authenticity, empowerment, and peer pressure affect us in our daily lives.

The Impact of Our Human Heritage

As descendants of primates, we have inherited a hierarchical nature and the tendency to imitate. Thus, we are predisposed to need both leadership and followership. Early socialization and the exposure to both positive and negative role models also affect an individual's self-definition, future behavior, and identification with groups of like-minded individuals. By the age of five, a child "already has a sense of himself and of other individuals, as persons and as members of the group" (Gardner, 1995). Although it is true that a leader cannot lead without followers, leadership and followership are both parts of our nature. It is important to remember that the ability of leaders to inspire others develops after they have recognized their own identity.

Self-awareness begins in childhood but should be considered a lifelong process of ongoing discovery and improvement. According to Kate Boyd Dernocoeur (1996), an experienced paramedic and lecturer/author of EMS topics, "educating yourself about your past and what it did to you can help you understand your reactions to what you see in EMS." I believe her position applies to both providers and leaders. Understanding who you are, where you have been, and where you want to go will provide a solid foundation on which to build your career as an EMS leader.

Motivation

Historically, motivation has been categorized as intrinsic or extrinsic. Edward Deci, a professor of psychology at the University of Rochester, has studied human motivation for more than three decades. He suggests that people perform intrinsically motivated behaviors for two reasons: to achieve stimulation and to achieve a sense of accomplishment, competence, and mastery over their environment (as cited in Lefton, 1991). Extrinsic motivators, on the other hand, would include such things as recognition, an excellent performance review, pay, and other "rewards." The challenge for EMS leaders becomes identifying which of their people respond to the intrinsic versus the extrinsic and the potential impact that the receipt or lack of one may have over the other. Thomas S. Pittman of Colby University and Jack S. Heller of Franklin and Marshall College, who both studied various aspects of human motivation, caution that "when extrinsic rewards are given in such a way that will alter a person's motivational orientation, they can decrease intrinsic motivation" (as cited in Lefton, 1991). In the ever-evolving world in which we live and work, leaders must take the time and make the extra effort to better understand the needs and aspirations of their people. By making this deeper connection, rather than simply using a traditional reward-and-punishment approach, leaders will be better able to provide motivation and increase the desire to succeed. Having an understanding of the different types of motivation and their effects on others is an important part of leadership.

Needs Theories

There have been many theories of how fulfilling and not fulfilling certain needs affects an individual's behavior. Perhaps the most well-known of these theories is Maslow's hierarchy of needs, which addresses psychological, safety, social, esteem, and self-actualization needs. These five areas are further categorized into lower-order and higher-order needs with the lower-order taking precedence over the higher-order needs. For example, Maslow believed that the necessities of life (food, water, shelter) must be addressed before someone will focus on higher-order needs like friendships, acceptance, and socialization.

Other needs theories are Alderfer's ERG theory, which effectively categorized the hierarchy into three areas: existence, relatedness, and growth; Herzberg's motivational theory, which focuses on motivators (intrinsic) and hygiene (extrinsic) factors; and McClelland's needs theory, which emphasizes achievement, affiliation, and power. Although each approaches the concept in its own way, at the core of each of the theories is the common belief that when various needs are not met, an individual will be unhappy, and the individual's behavior will be less desirable.

According to the Dalai Lama, as translated by Zelie Pollon, "once our most immediate needs are satisfied, our notion of happiness changes slightly and the means of obtaining it becomes more complicated" (Dresser, 1995). The important point about needs theories for the EMS leader to remember is that there are a variety of factors that can both motivate and frustrate people. Understanding this and focusing on the things that motivate you and your people while doing your best to avoid the areas that tend to erode satisfaction and motivation is a critical element of leading people.

Comparing the Components of Various Needs Theories

Maslow	Herzberg		Alderfer	McClelland
	Motivators (Intrinsic)	**Hygiene Factors (Extrinsic)**		
Self-actualization Esteem Social Safety Psychological	Achievement Recognition Challenge Responsibility Growth Development	Policies & Procedures Working Conditions Relationships Quality of Supervision Pay Benefits	Existence Relatedness Growth	Achievement Affiliation Power

Source: Second Class Petty Officer Leadership Course Student Guide (Chief of Naval Education and Training, 1996).

> **"***An authentic person is genuine and does not feign qualities or beliefs that he/she does not actually possess.***"**
>
> –Weichun Zhu, Douglas R. May, and Bruce J. Avolino, authors of
> "The Impact of Ethical Behavior on Employee Outcomes,"
> *Journal of Leadership and Organizational Studies*

Factors Contributing to the Development of Trust

- Communication
- Support
- Respect
- Fairness
- Credibility
- Competence
- Consistency

Source: Leaders, Fools and Imposters (Kets de Vries, 2003).

Authenticity

In the simplest of terms, authenticity is about being real. For EMS leaders, transparency and authenticity are essential for success. One's effectiveness and ability to lead are greatly affected by the consistency between statements and actions. Inconsistency breeds mistrust and strips away earned authority, whereas consistency breeds a positive environment in which followers know what to expect from their leaders. One of the simplest yet most damaging ways a leader can be perceived as disingenuous is by failing to follow up on a promised action. This situation will result in a disappointed follower and diminished trust in the leader's future promises. Being authentic in words and deeds will go a long way toward establishing and maintaining trust between leaders and followers.

Empowerment

When people feel empowered, they are more likely to be committed to their organization and to have trust in their leaders. "By definition, empowered employees are more likely to see themselves as competent and able to influence their job and organizations in a meaningful way" (Zhu et al., 2004). In EMS, providers of all levels are accustomed to working independently with their partners under protocols or standing orders that reinforce their scope of practice and define their agency's standard of care. Given this dynamic of the EMS workforce, it is important for EMS leaders to realize that their people work best when provided the tools and guidance to do their job and then are left alone to function without their superiors. This is not always possible, but empowering EMS personnel to do their jobs independently builds critical thinking skills and trust. In short, leadership through empowerment is about bringing out the best in people.

> **"***A tension will always exist between those who use their knowledge to manipulate and those who use their knowledge to empower.***"**
>
> –Howard Gardner, author of *Leading Minds*

Leadership Through the Hollywood Lens

In *The General's Daughter* (West, 1999), the investigation into the murder of Army Captain Elizabeth Campbell (played by Leslie Stefanson) uncovers a number of instances in which power and influence were used to manipulate a subordinate into ignoring malicious acts instead of acting legally, ethically, and morally. The investigation begins with Lieutenant General Joseph Campbell, father of the murdered Captain Campbell, and his adjutant, Colonel George Fowler (Clarence Williams III), attempting to exert influence over Warrant Officer Paul Brenner (John Travolta). In their first meeting, the General states that Brenner will have to choose between his roles as a loyal soldier and as a police officer, revealing the General's belief that the two were different and that somehow, based upon his own experiences, choosing the role of loyal soldier over police officer would be a better fit with the outcome he desires for the investigation. As Brenner and his partner, Sara Sunhill (Madeleine Stowe), leave the meeting, Colonel Fowler asks that they notify him of any contemplated arrests before they are made. As the investigation unfolds, Brenner and Sunhill discover that years ago, General Campbell was pressured by his superiors and, for the "good of the Army," encouraged his daughter, Captain Campbell, to refrain from reporting that she had been sexually assaulted during a military training exercise. The suppression of this incident appears to have bolstered the General's career, but was detrimental to his daughter's mental health and ultimately led to her murder. Having been manipulated earlier in his career very likely encouraged General Campbell to engage in similarly manipulative tactics with Brenner and Sunhill in the case of his daughter's murder.

In EMS, leaders of an organization are most often groomed and promoted from within the ranks. As we discussed in Chapter 1, making the transition from peer to superior is not often easy. In fact, former peers often will attempt to use their "friendship connection" with a superior to curry special favor regarding anything from scheduling to special details to help in avoiding disciplinary action. On the flip side, superiors are challenged with the temptation to misuse their influence with former peers and even to ask them to ignore issues that might otherwise result in negative consequences for someone the superior wishes to protect, or even to protect themselves. Using existing relationships to achieve the goals of an organization is beneficial to leaders in any endeavor. However, we must realize that the gray area is often defined only by one's moral compass and that leaders and followers will both be challenged by ethical decisions in both public and private situations.

> **"**An organizational culture will depend very much on the kind of psychological contract that exists between leader and followers.**"**
>
> –Manfred F. R. Kets de Vries, author of *Leaders, Fools, and Imposters*

Manipulation

According to Gardner (1995), "a tension will always exist between those who use their knowledge to manipulate and those who use their knowledge to empower." Understanding and accepting this fact will help us realize just how sacred a trust leaders hold. Leaders can use their knowledge and power for good or evil. "[W]hen a shared social identity exists, individuals who can best represent that identity will have the most influence over the group's members and be the most effective leaders" (Reicher, Platow, & Haslam, 2007). Therefore, in EMS, the people who connect best with staff will likely be the most effective in leading them. A challenge exists when staff members or leaders have a personal agenda that undermines the organization, and their ability to influence the group is stronger than the influence of staff or leaders who wish to succeed in a more positive way. Effectively, this is an earned authority with the group. However, with this connection and earned authority can come the power to manipulate, and this reinforces the importance of ethics for the leader and staff member alike.

Conformity

In his article "The Man Who Shocked the World," Thomas Blass (2002) cites an experiment that law professor Steven Hartwell conducted with his students at the University of San Diego. For the experiment, law students were instructed to advise clients in a small claims court rent dispute to lie under oath. The goal was to place students in a position that forced them to choose between obedience to authority and ethically correct behavior. Although some expressed an objection or concern, 23 of 24 students advised the clients (who Hartwell had hired) to perjure themselves. The results clearly show that, as followers, we must guard against giving in to improper orders, and, as leaders, we must be sure to foster in our followers the ability to think and act independently.

Power Motives, Narcissism, and Servant Leadership

To be an effective leader, a strong need for power is perhaps desirable; however, one must look at the underlying motivation. Gary Yukl (2006), in his text *Leadership in Organizations*, reminds us that "the empirical research has indicated that a socialized power orientation is more likely to result in effective leadership than a personalized power orientation." Those with personalized power orientation use power to satisfy their own need for esteem and status, whereas those with a socialized power orientation tend to be more mature and exercise power for the benefit of others.

Given the traits associated with narcissism, it is likely that those who have such a personality will be found aspiring to and serving in positions of authority. According to Yukl (2006), "narcissism refers to a personality syndrome that involves an extreme need for esteem (e.g., prestige, status, attention, admiration, and adulation), a strong need for power, weak self control, and indifference about the needs and welfare of others." Additionally, they "tend to surround themselves with subordinates who are loyal and uncritical." You will recall that in Chapter 2 we looked at a

Leadership Lessons from History

In an experiment conducted at Yale University, psychologist Stanley Milgram measured the willingness of study participants to obey an authority figure when instructed to perform an act that conflicted with their consciences. The experiment tested how much pain an ordinary citizen would inflict on another person simply because he was ordered to do so by an experimental scientist. The goal was to test the power of authority against the moral imperative to refrain from inflicting hurt on others. Ultimately, authority won more often than morality. In a 1974 article entitled "The Perils of Obedience" (as cited in Graham, 2008), Milgram writes, "[t]he extreme willingness of adults to go to almost any lengths on the command of an authority constitutes the chief finding of the study and the fact most urgently demanding explanation." In his experiment, according to the American Psychological Association (2004), "[d]espite the learner's increasingly pitiful screams and pleas to stop, a majority of subjects (more than 60%) obeyed the experimenter's commands to continue and ended up giving the maximum 'shock' of 450 volts." This tells us not necessarily just that people have a tendency to follow orders, but that people are inclined to do things that they may not otherwise do if they believe that an authority figure is taking responsibility for their actions as well as defining what is proper and improper behavior under a given set of circumstances.

EMS personnel and their leaders are placed in high regard by the public, and a sacred trust is inherent in their roles as public safety professionals. Understanding the potential implication of Milgram's experiment as it relates to human behavior will provide the EMS leader with the knowledge to recognize and minimize, if not eliminate, the occurrences of improper behavior that take advantage of human susceptibility.

variety of leadership styles, and in Chapter 1 we explored the desire to lead. With this background in mind we can gain insight into what drives us and the leaders around us. Dr. Michael McCoby of Harvard (as cited in Gerstel, 2001) believes that a form of productive narcissism exists and that "all visionary leaders are narcissistic personalities." As with everything else in life, we must take the good with the bad and realize that although there may be positives associated with narcissism, we want to look at the traits exhibited by those in leadership positions and their effect on the people and organization around them.

In stark contrast to narcissistic leadership styles, servant leaders find individuals who empower their followers instead of using power to dominate or control them. Trust plays a key role in the effectiveness of the servant leader and, according to Yukl, trust is established by "being completely honest and open, keeping actions consistent with values, and showing trust in followers." When you think about the old expression that actions speak louder than words and apply it to the leader–follower relationship, it is clear that the impact of leading by example is a key element in building an atmosphere of trust. In EMS today, personnel tend to respond favorably to leaders who hold themselves accountable and to the same, if not a higher, standard of behavior as their subordinates. Conversely, personnel who see the "do as I say, not as I do" approach tend to mistrust leaders. Clearly, given the environment in which we work, the servant leadership style and the individuals who practice it have an established place in EMS.

You Are the EMS Leader

Two of your EMTs come to you after having made some mistakes in the care of a patient who is related to a member of your organization. A few weeks later, the member who is related to this patient raises the incident at your organization's monthly meeting and asks what actions have been taken as a result of the mistakes and what can be done in the future to avoid similar problems.

1. Given that you already had knowledge of the incident, how would you respond to the individual now raising the matter at your meeting?

2. Would the fact that you chose to take or not to take corrective action with respect to the performance of the EMTs in question change your approach to the question? Why or why not?

3. Would you address the matter differently based on your personal relationships with the people involved? Why or why not?

> **"** *Most people will experience temporary periods of burnout or imbalance . . . long periods of imbalance can be dangerous to your health, destructive to your relationships and can endanger your job."*
>
> –Jim Bouchard, author of *Dynamic Components of Personal Power*

Stress and Burnout

The reality of the EMS profession is that there is inherent stress present every day for providers and leaders alike. Understanding that stress exists and developing a healthy approach to it will minimize the negative physical, psychological, and emotional consequences that often accompany poorly managed stress. A significant result of the effects of stress is burnout. As an EMS leader you are responsible not only for avoiding and coping with your own stress, but you must also do your best to minimize and respond to the impact of stress on your people. It is vitally important to recognize the kinds of situations and events that can create stress as well as the signs and symptoms of stress in your providers.

Language of Leadership

- **Burnout**—Occurs when coping mechanisms no longer buffer job stressors, which can compromise personal health and well-being
- **Stress**—Any event or situation that places extraordinary demands on a person's mental or emotional resources
- **Stressor**—An emotional stimulus that affects an organism in ways that are physically or psychologically injurious, usually producing anxiety, tension, and/or psychological arousal

Common Causes of Stress in EMS

Occupational Stressors
- Long or extended shifts
- Too much overtime
- Conflicts (value conflicts, management or bureaucratic conflicts)
- Interpersonal problems (with supervisors, instructors, physicians)
- Incompetent partners, poor peer support
- Poor advancement opportunities
- Poor system designs
- Poor pay or other compensation
- Little recognition
- Job burnout
- Insufficient budget
- Life and death issues

- Maintaining emotional neutrality with victims and perpetrators
- Hazardous work conditions
- Mass-casualty incidents
- Threats of terrorism
- Dealing with the media
- Expectations of the public
- Overeager citizens with police scanners
- Obstructive people
- Fear of inadequate training or not enough training
- Poor professional communication skills
- Too many charity events (pancake breakfasts, bean suppers, car washes)
- Not enough action

Personal Stressors
- Lack of high-quality family time
- Lack of personal time
- Marital problems

- Financial difficulties
- Car problems, traffic
- Personal health concerns

Adapted from: Managing Stress in Emergency Medical Services (Seaward, 2000).

Common Warning Signs and Symptoms of Stress

- Irritability toward coworkers, family, and friends
- Inability to concentrate
- Difficulty sleeping, increased sleeping, or nightmares
- Anxiety
- Indecisiveness
- Guilt
- Loss of appetite (gastrointestinal disturbances)
- Loss of interest in sexual activities
- Isolation
- Loss of interest in work
- Increased use of alcohol
- Recreational drug use

Source: Emergency Care and Transportation of the Sick and Injured, Ninth edition (Pollak et al., 2005).

Anatomy of a True Apology

- Admitting fault
- Showing remorse
- Acknowledging damage
- Indicating how it will be repaired

Source: Contrition as Leadership (Quindlen, 2007).

The Apology

In Chapter 4, we discussed the power of "thank you" in the interpersonal connection between leaders and followers. Here, we look at the psychological importance of an apology by leaders who have made a mistake, overstepped their bounds, or otherwise negatively affected their people or organization. According to Thom Dick (2005), "[t]here's great power in humility." Additionally, he writes, "humility is not the same as pretending to be less than you are. That's phony. Humility is honesty—acknowledging the contributions of those around you, along with your own—and acknowledging your weaknesses." The ability of a leader to accept responsibility for a mistake and take the time to apologize, especially to subordinates, speaks volumes to character and will build a relationship of trust between the leader and followers.

"If power means never having to say you're sorry, then the powerful miss the opportunity to truly lead."

–Anna Quindlen, author of *Contrition as Leadership*

Wrap-Up

Chapter Summary

In this chapter, we looked at the roots of leadership and followership that exist in our common human heritage as well as intrinsic and extrinsic motivators to both lead and follow. Through examples like *The General's Daughter*, we considered power motives, manipulation, and providing empowerment. An examination of the experiments of Steven Hartwell and Stanley Milgram showed that the influence of authority can be very powerful and that leaders and followers alike must be cautious and vigilant so that they do not improperly use influence as it relates to conformity. Finally, we discussed the value of humility and the power of the apology. Our study of the basics of how psychology affects leaders and followers should serve as both a foundation for our practice of leadership and a stepping-off point for further study of psychology as it relates to leadership in EMS.

Why Their Views Matter: About the Individuals Cited in the Chapter

Clayton P. Alderfer served on the faculty of the Rutgers University Graduate School of Applied and Professional Psychology and the Yale School of Organization and Management. He is well known for his ERG motivational theory and is the founder of Alderfer and Associates, which provides support and consulting services to the private, nonprofit, and public sectors.

Thomas Blass is a professor of psychology at the University of Maryland, Baltimore County. Among his works are a biography of Stanley Milgram and the website www.stanleymilgram.com.

Jim Bouchard is a motivational speaker and author of *Dynamic Components of Personal Power*. He has studied martial arts since 1985 and was inducted into the U.S. Martial Arts Hall of Fame in 2004. Both in his book and in his seminars, Bouchard focuses on personal development, entrepreneurship, and employee motivation.

The Dalai Lama is the head of state and spiritual leader of the Tibetan people. He has lived in exile in India since fleeing the Chinese occupation of his country in 1959. He is perhaps one of the most prominent Buddhist leaders in the world and supports peaceful activism and compassion.

Edward L. Deci is professor of psychology and director of the human motivation program at the University of Rochester. He holds a PhD in psychology from Carnegie-Mellon University.

Thom Dick has been a passionate advocate of EMS patients and their caregivers for more than 35 years. Thom spent more than 23 years as an EMT and paramedic in San Diego County. He is the author of a number of monthly columns in several EMS journals. He is a well-known international speaker and the coauthor of the book *People Care: Career Friendly Practices for Professional Caregivers*.

Kate Boyd Dernocoeur has been involved in EMS since 1973. Over the years she has lectured extensively in the United States and Canada. She worked as a paramedic in Denver City and Denver County. She is the author of *Streetsense: Communication, Safety, and Control* and coauthor of *Principles of Emergency Medical Dispatch*.

Howard Gardner is a professor of education at the Harvard Graduate School of Education. He is also an adjunct professor of neurology at Boston University. He is the author of more than a dozen books, including *The Unschooled Mind: How Children Think and How Schools Should Teach*.

Steven Hartwell is a professor of law at the University of San Diego. He received his JD from the University of Southern California. He has been widely published and teaches negotiation, interviewing, and counseling as well as professional responsibility.

S. Alexander Haslam is a professor of social psychology at the University of Exeter. He received his PhD from Macquarie University in Sydney, Australia. Before coming to the University of Exeter, he spent 10 years at the Australian National University in Canberra.

Jack F. Heller holds a PhD from the University of Iowa. His research interests include interpersonal relations and social motivation. He is an associate professor of psychology at Franklin and Marshall College.

Frederick I. Herzberg is perhaps best known for his theory on motivation. He graduated from the City College of New York after serving in the U.S. Army. He completed his PhD at the University of Pittsburgh and served as a professor of psychology at Case Western Reserve University and as a professor of management at the University of Utah.

Manfred F. R. Kets de Vries is a Professor of Clinical Leadership at INSEAD and the author, coauthor, or editor of more than 24 books.

Lester A. Lefton is president of Kent State University and has more than 35 years of experience in higher education. Among his many positions, he served as director of graduate studies in general experimental psychology at the University of South Carolina. He has published dozens of research articles and is the author of *Psychology*.

Abraham Maslow received his PhD in psychology from the University of Wisconsin. He is the author of numerous articles and a number of books, including *Toward a Psychology of Being, Motivation and Personality*, and *The Further Reaches of Human Nature*. He taught at Brooklyn College and was the chairman of the Psychology Department at Brandeis University.

David C. McClelland was a distinguished research professor of psychology at Boston University and professor emeritus at Harvard University. Much of his work centered on human needs and motivation. He held a doctorate in psychology from Yale University.

Michael McCoby holds a PhD from Harvard University and is president of the McCoby Group. He has consulted for, among others, AT&T and the U.S. Department of State. He is the author of numerous books, including *The Leaders We Need: And What Makes Us Follow* and *Narcissistic Leaders: Who Succeeds and Who Fails*.

Stanley Milgram received a PhD in social psychology from Harvard. While an assistant professor at Yale, Milgram conducted experiments on the power of social influence. He later returned to Harvard as an assistant professor in the Department of Social Relations and after 3 years in that position moved to the City University of New York as a full professor and head of the social psychology program for its graduate center.

Ross Perot is a leader in American business and political circles. Widely known for his 1992 independent run for the White House, he is the founder of Electronic Data Systems, Perot Systems, and the Reform Party.

Thomas S. Pittman is a professor and chair of the psychology department at Colby College in Waterville, Maine. He holds a PhD in social psychology from the University of Iowa.

Michael J. Platow is an associate professor at the Australian National University School of Psychology. Previously he worked at the School of Psychological Science at La Trobe University in Melbourne and in the Department of Psychology at the University of Otago in New Zealand. He holds a doctorate from the University of California, Santa Barbara.

Anna Quindlen was a columnist at the *New York Times* from 1981 to 1984. She has been published in numerous newspapers and magazines. In 1992 she received a Pulitzer Prize for Commentary, and in 1993 a collection of her columns was published by Random House.

Stephen D. Reicher is professor of social psychology at the University of Saint Andrews. He received his PhD from the University of Bristol. Before moving to the University of Saint Andrews, he held positions at the University of Dundee and the University of Exeter. Much of his work over the years has focused on leadership and topics such as crowd behavior and tyranny.

Gary Yukl holds a PhD from the University of California at Berkeley and is a professor at the State University of New York at Albany. He is the author of the text *Leadership in Organizations*, which focuses on effective leadership in organizations through both theory and practice. His book combines theory and his research on leadership, providing an insightful look at the use of power and how its components can influence the behavior of subordinates and peers.

Weichun Zhu is Senior Research Fellow of the Kravis Leadership Institute at Claremont McKenna College. He previously served as a visiting scholar at the School of Public Policy and Management at Tsinghua University in China. He holds a PhD from the University of Nebraska at Lincoln. In addition to coauthoring "The Impact of Ethical Behavior on Employee Outcomes" in the *Journal of Leadership and Organizational Studies* with Douglas R. May and Bruce J. Avolino, he is the author of numerous research works and book chapters and has made numerous presentations at conferences around the world.

Chapter 7

Mentoring and Subordinate Development

❚❚ The ultimate leader is one who is willing to develop people to the point that they surpass him or her in knowledge and ability. **❚❚**

—Fred A. Manske

Introduction

In *The Magic of 3 A.M.*, Jim Page writes, "I've always enjoyed the opportunity to help bright young people meet their occupational or professional goals." To many of us, Jim Page was the consummate mentor, and his contributions will forever change the people whose lives he touched. Jim knew the importance of mentoring and developing others to improve themselves, their organizations, and the EMS industry. That was his gift to us, and as EMS leaders, our gift, in fact our obligation, to our people is to be the best mentors we can be to help them achieve their greatest potential.

The Leader as Mentor

With all the challenges and priorities facing EMS leaders today, it is easy to overlook the intangible importance of mentoring your people. "It is always easier to dismiss a man than it is to train him. No great leader ever built a reputation on firing people. Many have built a reputation on developing them" (anonymous, as cited in Pockell & Avila, 2007). Placing the development of your people at the top of your permanent list of priorities will serve you, your organization, and your subordinates in the long run. For example, delegation is often thought of simply as a leadership or management tool to accomplish tasks. However, if delegation is used correctly, it can also be a personnel and organizational development tool. Through delegation, leaders and managers not only free up their time but they also develop their professional skills within their own positions and develop an

Language of Leadership

- **Mentor**–A trusted counselor or guide
- **Protégé**–A person guided and helped, especially in the furtherance of his or her career, by another, more influential person
- **Preceptor**–A teacher or tutor
- **Trainee**–One that is being trained, especially for a job
- **Field training officer (FTO)**–An experienced or senior member of an organization who is responsible for the training of a junior or probationary level member

ability to let go of certain tasks while at the same time building their ability to trust their people to get the job done. For the people to whom tasks and responsibilities are delegated, there are opportunities to learn and to grow. Additionally, they will feel empowered and more connected to their leaders, managers, and organization. They also will have a sense of ownership of the project and, as a result, a deeper commitment is established. As a leader you must not only direct your people in their daily tasks, but you must guide, nurture, and cultivate them not only to do their jobs better but to succeed you and become the leaders of the future.

Delegation as a Personnel Development Tool

- Direction is provided to the employee as to what needs to be done.
- Empower the employee to accomplish the task or project.
- Learn through doing the task or project.
- Encourage growth and development.
- Gauge how it's going.
- Accountability is learned by the protégé, but ultimately responsibility for completion rests with the mentor.
- Train on areas needed to complete the task or project and step in as needed.
- Evaluate progress and results.

Typical Roles of the Mentor

- **Coach**–Demonstrate how to carry out a task or activity
- **Facilitator**–Create opportunities for learners to use newly acquired skills
- **Counselor**–Help protégé explore the consequences of potential decision
- **Networker**–Refer protégé to others when the mentor's own experience is insufficient

Source: Paying It Forward: The Importance of Being a Mentor (Barishansky, 2006).

The Mentoring Relationship

According to McCauley and Van Velsor (2004), "a mentoring relationship is typically defined as a committed long-term relationship in which a senior person (mentor) supports the personal and professional development of a junior person (protégé)." The concept of the mentor–protégé relationship is not foreign to EMS; in fact, variations on the theme have been used during EMT and paramedic training and orientation for years in the form of preceptors and field training officers (FTOs). In the cases of preceptors and FTOs, the connection is there, but it is limited to a shorter-term purpose, such as clinical time as part of training or a new employee's orientation, or perhaps remediation of an identified clinical or behavioral issue. A mentoring relationship reaches beyond a singular short-term goal to the overall growth and development of the individual in both career and life.

The Role of the Mentor

To be an effective mentor one must value the development of others and be willing to make the necessary commitment of time and energy to establish and maintain a meaningful mentor–protégé relationship. The mentor must be able to actively listen and provide both knowledge and support to the protégé without providing all the solutions. Mentors must be sounding boards that allow the protégé to explore thoughts and challenges. Mentors exist to provide the insight, opinion, and support that protégés can use to develop themselves and their approach to overcoming any obstacles. Mentors also have the responsibility to provide their views of any potential consequences they foresee as a result of a protégé's plans or actions. The mentor must confront the protégé in a positive and meaningful way with any constructive criticism. Mentors should not micromanage but rather should listen, guide, trust, and share in the protégé's curiosity and embrace the learning environment they share.

The Role of the Protégé

In the mentor–protégé relationship, the protégé must be an active participant to gain the most from the encounter. Protégés must make their needs and desires known and they must take responsibility for their own self-improvement, growth, and development. They need to set realistic goals and objectives and must be open to feedback and constructive criticism from the mentor. The protégé needs to contribute ideas and with the support of the mentor develop plans to achieve their goals. The protégé must

> **"***Mentors need an attitude of being lifelong learners and must understand that mentoring is an opportunity to develop leadership skills in themselves and those they mentor.***"**
>
> —Greg Schaffer, Speaker, EMS Expo 2006

remember that the mentor is there to provide guidance, but not necessarily the answers. In short, the protégé must help manage the relationship as part of the process in order to gain the most from it.

The Impact of Mentoring

Research has shown that "in contrast to those who have not received mentoring, protégés have greater opportunities, higher compensation, and receive more promotions" (Fagenson, 1989; Scandura, 1992; Whitney et al., 1991, as cited in Forret & de Janasz, 2005). Given these proven benefits, it is clear that the support of mentoring in EMS organizations will enhance growth opportunities for the providers of today and the leaders of tomorrow.

The effect of mentoring on the protégé is clear, but it is important to realize that there are also profound benefits to leaders who take on the role of mentor, either formally or informally. Mentors have the unique opportunity to learn, grow, and develop their own coaching, listening, and leadership skills while putting their time and energy into the development of others and the improvement of their overall organization.

Creating a Positive Culture of Support

An organization's ability to create an atmosphere of trust that supports both the personal and professional growth of its people while working toward achieving balance between work and family is essential for the success of the organization and its employees. Authors Dan Carrison and Rod Walsh of *Business Leadership the Marine Corps Way*, both served in the U.S. Marine Corps and provide their insights on why the Corps have such success: "From Day One at boot camp—even before, in the recruiting office—the young recruit is told that he will soon be a member of the greatest fighting organization on the face of the earth. A hundred times a day, from every mouth that speaks, he hears how special he is." Carrison and Walsh remind us that "[t]here is something to be said for constant positive reinforcement." When people get up each day and look forward to going to work not only because their job is their chosen profession, but also because the atmosphere lends itself to increased job satisfaction, commitment and performance will improve. Additionally, the likelihood of burnout and excessive absenteeism will decrease.

Coaching

When the topic of coaching is raised we often think of sports. Whether at the highest levels of professional sports like the National Football League

---

Benefits to the Protégé

- Career development
- Challenging work
- Coaching
- Sponsorship
- Exposure and visibility
- Protection
- Guidance
- Confirmation
- Acceptance
- Friendship
- Counseling

Source: Perceptions of an Organization's Culture for Work and Family: Do Mentors Make a Difference? (Forret & de Janasz, 2005).

Benefits to the Mentor

- Obtain a greater understanding of the barriers experienced at lower levels of the organization
- Enhance their own skills in coaching, counseling, listening, and modeling
- Gain a sense of being needed and recognized professionally
- Develop and practice a more personal style of leadership
- Gain additional recognition and respect
- Learn new perspectives and approaches
- Contribute something to others in the organization
- Extend professional networks
- Demonstrate expertise and share knowledge

Source: Mentoring: A Discussion Paper (Wareing et al., 2007).

and Major League Baseball or at the college, high school, or Little League levels, the coach teaches the players the skills needed to perform well in their positions and as part of the team. Like mentoring, coaching involves a mutual sharing of experiences and opinions to facilitate the desired outcomes. The coach is the person who helps others improve and the one to whom they turn when in a slump. Patty McManus, author of *Coaching People* (2006), tells us that coaching works best when "you coach or ask to be coached when you believe that working together will lead to improved performance." Coaching provides a catalyst for learning and a way of guiding people toward their goals.

Giving and Receiving Feedback

Providing feedback to personnel is a central role of leadership. In the mentor–protégé relationship, its importance is even greater and therefore must become a well-honed skill for the mentor. When preparing to give feedback, it is important to examine both your motivations and the desired outcome. When possible, select a time and a place that will facilitate the protégé's openness to what you have to say. I say "when possible" because there will be times, such as during emergency situations, when immediate feedback is required to correct or overcome something that cannot wait for a retrospective discussion. When giving feedback it is also important to focus on the behavior and your perceptions of it and to separate the behavior from the individual. Of equal if not greater importance is allowing the protégé an opportunity to receive, consider, and respond to your concerns. It is the mentor's job to allow the protégé to consider, clarify, and explain his or her position and perspective in an environment where it is safe to do so without fear of ridicule or reprisal.

When asking for feedback as a leader and a mentor, it is important that you are open to hearing information that may alter your perception or be flat-out critical. It is also important to remember that whether you agree or not, the feelings of the person providing feedback to you are real as is his or her perception of the situation. Finally, it is important for you to clarify your understanding, ask necessary questions, and take the time to discuss your positions and perceptions to ensure a better understanding for everyone involved.

Leadership Lessons from History

On September 11, 2001, Chief of Department Peter J. Ganci was among the 343 members of the New York City Fire Department who perished in the attacks on the World Trade Center. Side-by-side with his people, he provided courageous leadership until his untimely end. In fact, it has been said that "with the collapse of the second tower, the top command structure of the fire department of New York ceased to exist" (Golway, 2002), because along with him, Chief Raymond Downey and First Deputy Fire Commissioner William Feehan also perished. And yet, although decades of knowledge and experience were lost, the FDNY leadership did not actually cease to exist; it was simply altered by the tragedy. No agency was specifically prepared for the tragic events of September 11, and the importance of strong leadership development and a succession plan has never been tested as violently and abruptly. The leaders who took command after the loss of their superiors honored their memory, their service, and their sacrifice by being well-prepared and able to apply all that their predecessors had passed down to them.

You Are
the EMS Leader

You are elected to take over a position in a small EMS agency, where your responsibilities include scheduling and supplies. The person to whom you report is not pleased with your selection for this position and in fact had been taking on the responsibilities of the position in addition to his own for quite some time. When you seek his guidance and direction for how to proceed with your duties, you are brushed aside. Eventually, you are told that supplies can be ordered only after this person approves the order, and the order must be shipped to his attention. You are given no guidance whatsoever about the schedule, although many people, yourself included, have been unhappy with how the schedule has been handled in the past.

After discussing some new ideas with other members of the organization, at the first meeting of the year you bring copies of the ideas to the table and encourage members to provide input and critique in the hope that sparking such openness will result in a more comprehensive finished product: a schedule that works better for more people. Based on the meeting's discussions and input received from others not at the meeting, you put together a new scheduling policy that is approved, albeit not unanimously, at the next meeting.

1. *How do you think the strained relationship between you and the senior officer will affect your individual and combined abilities to meet the respective responsibilities of your positions?*

2. *In retrospect, how could you have handled the scheduling issue differently?*

3. *If the new scheduling policy had been approved but your superior continued to undermine both it and your implementation of it, how would you as the junior officer address the situation?*

4. *Your term of office is up and you are not seeking to continue in the post. Your successor has been elected and will take over in 3 weeks.*

   a. *What guidance would you provide?*

   b. *Would you share any of the negative aspects of your interactions with your superior? Why or why not? If so, how much would you share?*

5. *What lessons could you take away from an experience like this that would be beneficial to you in future leadership roles?*

Role Modeling

When we think back on our lives, we can likely identify a number of key role models, both good and bad, who have affected us and contributed to who we are today. Our parents, our older siblings, aunts, uncles, teachers, coaches, and bosses have undoubtedly changed our lives. As leaders in our chosen field of EMS, we must also consider that we will affect the lives of people for years to come. According to Ari D. Kaplan, a "true leader inspires others to lead themselves" (as cited in Roberts, 2002). As the people charged with the development of others, we must prepare them to carry the torch of leadership in EMS so that our legacy lives on and EMS is left better off for our part in its development.

Being a positive role model and surrounding yourself with others of the same character and caliber is important to the reinforcement of the behaviors and mindsets that EMS leaders must possess. In contrast, Lorin Woolfe, who spent most of his life studying both leadership and the Bible, provides a powerful perspective for us to consider. In his book *Leadership Secrets from the Bible*, he tells us that "holding up an unethical person (no matter how successful) or an incompetent person (no matter how ethical) as a role model will only result in cynicism." If your behavior is seen as negative or inconsistent, you will reinforce the belief that this is acceptable, but if you remain positive and are consistent in your words and deeds, your people will look up to you and be more likely both to follow and to emulate you.

Succession Planning

One of your first priorities as a leader is to prepare your replacement to take over for you, in both the short term and the long term. In fact, according to Chief Dennis Wolf of the Germantown (Tennessee) Fire Department, "it is the implicit duty of every officer to prepare subordinates to

Leadership Through the Hollywood Lens

Early in the movie *Men in Black* (Sonnenfeld, 1997), Agent K (played by Tommy Lee Jones) is faced with finding and training a new person for the Men in Black (MIB) when his long-time partner, Agent D (Richard Hamilton), decides it is time to retire. Agent K sets his sights on New York City police detective James Edwards (Will Smith), who he believes has the potential to be a successful member of the team. After Detective Edwards and a number of other potential candidates participate in a screening process, Agent K convinces his boss, Chief Zed (Rip Torn), that Edwards is the right candidate. Chief Zed agrees, and Agent K sits down with his future protégé to spell out honestly and completely what will be expected of him should he decide to make the commitment. Once processed into MIB, Detective James Edwards takes on the new identity of Agent J. His training progresses through a series of encounters in which Agent K both provides direction and allows Agent J to make mistakes. Agent J's mistakes are then quickly used as catalysts for learning. The movie culminates with one final alien encounter that tests Agent J's new knowledge and abilities without the guidance of Agent K. After the encounter, Agent K informs Agent J that he has decided to retire. When J expresses concerns about losing his partner, K reassures him by saying, "I haven't been training a partner, I've been training a replacement."

take his or her place." With Chief Wolf's position in mind, consider the scenario in which you spent the last few years developing an organization or unit within an organization and have now been promoted or have left the organization entirely for an opportunity to advance your career. How would you feel if you returned a year later to find that the fruits of your labors had rotted away because the person who succeeded you failed to build on your foundation? If you move forward without preparing your replacement, you will have destroyed all your hard work and turned your long-term vision into a forgotten accomplishment.

Developing future leaders is not something that will take place overnight, but it is important to begin to cultivate an environment that will allow such development to exist and flourish. In his book *First In, Last Out: Leadership Lessons from the New York Fire Department*, John J. Salka refers to a leadership pipeline that is established by "developing leaders at all levels." Organizations vary in size and commitment to the selection and development of their people and their leaders. That said, and given the often fast-paced and chaotic environment in which EMS finds itself, it may well be difficult to allot the time and emphasis on leadership development that it deserves and requires. Therefore, EMS leaders should strive to build leadership development into the everyday bustle of their organizations through such things as delegation, mentoring, and—above all—creativity.

Traits to Consider in Selecting a Successor

- Leadership potential
- Ability and willingness to learn
- Ability to think conceptually and anticipate problems
- Adaptability and agility toward change
- Results oriented
- Fits the organizational culture

Source: Adapted from *Succession Planning—Mentoring and Educating Younger Fire Officers for the Chief's Position* (Wolf, 2006).

Wrap-Up

Chapter Summary

In this chapter, we discussed the roles of the mentor and the protégé and the important lessons and benefits each receives in the process. The value of a positive culture of mutual respect and support was addressed, along with the use of delegation and coaching for accomplishing tasks correctly while at the same time developing competent personnel and future leaders. From the newest recruit to the next in line for the department head position, the importance of providing staff with guidance and support for both the present and the future is invaluable in EMS. Many have the knowledge and potential to succeed, but they and the organizations in which they serve are far better off when there is a culture of cooperation that fosters the growth and development of everyone.

All too often in organizations of every shape and size the most valuable resources of all—the human resources—are often overlooked or taken for granted. By taking care of your people and encouraging them to learn and grow, you will prepare them to take care of themselves, their patients, their peers, and the organization. Whether formal or informal, mentoring helps develop the leaders of the future.

Why Their Views Matter: About the Individuals Cited in the Chapter

Raphael M. Barishansky is the executive director of the Hudson Valley (New York) Regional EMS Council. He holds a bachelor's degree in psychology from Touro College of Liberal Arts and Sciences and a master's degree in public health from New York Medical College. He is a site reviewer for the Commission on Accreditation of Ambulance Services (CAAS) and has served as a reviewer for the Continuing Education Coordinating Board for Emergency Medical Services (CECBEMS). He has an extensive writing background in EMS. His articles have been featured in *EMS Magazine*, *Journal of Emergency Medical Services*, *EMS Insider*, *EMS Manager and Supervisor*, and other publications.

Dan Carrison served in the U.S. Marine Corps and is a senior account executive for Diebold. He is coauthor of *Business Leadership the Marine Corps Way*.

Suzanne C. de Janasz holds a PhD from the University of Southern California and is a lecturer and general faculty member at the McIntire School of Commerce at the University of Virginia. She is the author of *Interpersonal Skills in Organizations* and of numerous articles relating to her specialty of organizational behavior, leadership, and interpersonal skills.

Monica Forret holds a PhD from the University of Missouri, and her expertise is in organizational behavior and human resource management. She is a professor at the St. Ambrose College of Business.

Fred A. Manske is author of the book *Secrets of Effective Leadership*.

Cynthia D. McCauley is a senior fellow at the Center for Creative Leadership. She is published in numerous professional journals, including the *Journal of Management*. She is coeditor of the *Handbook of Leadership Development*.

Patty McManus has provided leadership and organization development consulting to organizations for nearly 20 years. She has focused on developing collaborative change processes and skill in for-profit, public, and non-profit sectors. She served as an internal organizational development consultant for the University of California at Berkeley, Kaiser Permanente, and Apple Computer. She has an MS in industrial and organizational psychology from San Francisco State University.

James O. Page is the founder of JEMS Communications and the publisher emeritus of *Journal of Emergency Medical Services*. Before becoming an attorney and forming the law firm Page, Wolfberg, and Wirth, Jim began his career as a fire fighter in Los Angeles, where he played an instrumental role in the implementation of the paramedic program. He was also a consultant for the television show *Emergency* and was chief of EMS for the state of North Carolina. He is the author of a number of books, including *The Magic of 3 A.M.*

Wess Roberts is author of *The Best Advice Ever for Leaders* and *Leadership Secrets of Attila the Hun*. He earned his doctorate in psychology from Utah State University. He has worked with the U.S. Army, American Express Company, Fireman's Fund Insurance Company, and Northrop Services Company. Roberts has also instructed graduate and undergraduate students at Nova Southeastern University, Southern Utah University, and Utah State University. He has appeared on over 400 radio and television programs.

John J. Salka joined the New York City Fire Department in 1979 and rose through the ranks from fire fighter to lieutenant, captain, and battalion chief. As a battalion chief, he leads 30 officers and 150 fire fighters. In addition to his book *First In–Last Out: Leadership Lessons from the New York Fire Department*, he is the author of many articles in fire fighting and leadership techniques. He is also a nationally recognized speaker and has been featured at the Worcester Safety and Survival Seminar and many other seminars.

Greg Schaffer is a professional training consultant who specializes in emergency medical, fire, and emergency communications services. A certified instructor with over 25 years of experience in public safety, Schaffer is recognized nationally and has made over 200 public presentations including conferences and professional seminars. He is currently a fire and EMS captain and training manager in Atlanta, Georgia.

Ellen Van Velsor is a senior research scientist and a research-and-development director at the Center for Creative Leadership. She is coauthor of *Breaking the Glass Ceiling: Can Women Reach the Top of America's Largest Corporations?* and the coeditor of the *Handbook of Leadership Development*.

Rod Walsh served in the U.S. Marine Corps and is a Vietnam veteran. He holds an MBA and is coauthor of *Business Leadership the Marine Corps Way*.

Dennis Wolf is the chief of the Germantown (Tennessee) Fire Department. He joined the department in March 1977 and rose through the ranks to become fire chief in November 1995. He also serves as Germantown's emergency management director. He holds a BS degree in fire administration from the University of Memphis and an MS degree in fire service leadership from Grand Canyon University.

Lorin Woolfe has organized and delivered for Manufacturers Hanover Trust, E. F. Hutton, Deloitte, the Institute of Management Accountants, and others. He has also served as a specialist in leadership at the American Management Association and as Vice President of Program Development for Drake, Beam, Morin (DBM), a globally recognized career management firm. As a student of the Bible and religion most of his life, he combined his studies with his professional experiences and is the author of *The Bible on Leadership*.

8

The Leader's Role in Performance Improvement

> ❚❚If I had permitted my failures, or what seemed to me at the time to be a lack of success, to discourage me I cannot see any way in which I would have ever made progress. ❚❚
>
> —Calvin Coolidge

Introduction

Back in the 1980s, America was challenged by Japan's ability to manufacture products like cars and electronics of a better quality for a lower cost. Their culture of quality and the use of quality practices allowed them to compete profitably in the United States. When one calls 9-1-1, one is not offered a choice in responding agencies or personnel. Instead, the closest available unit is sent. John Becknell, publisher of *EMS Best Practices*, states that there are some who believe "we don't need to embrace quality improvement because most of us operate without much competition." Emergency services agencies and personnel will sometimes become complacent in the quality of their service. Since EMS agencies are not often challenged externally by competition, the motivation for quality performance and improvement must come from within. Although quality assurance and quality improvement (QA-QI) are overseen by the medical director and others in the executive suite, it is the EMS leader who must be the example and create a culture that embraces and embodies high-quality patient care and customer service.

Approaches to Quality

Among the pioneers in development of quality management and improvement in the United States was W. Edwards Deming, who began his work in Japan in the 1950s. Deming believed that "quality is maintained and improved when leaders, managers, and the workforce understand and commit to constant customer satisfaction through continuous quality improvement" (Eastham & Champion, 1997). Deming and a colleague put forth a plan–do–check–act (PDCA) approach. The PDCA cycle is continuous and begins with a plan or policy. The policy is implemented, checked periodically, and solidified or modified as needed based on its effectiveness. Like everything else in EMS, there is no magic bullet or single solution that will fix or address every problem or situation, and therefore Eastham and Champion (1997) remind us that "the dramatic improvements of the initial PDCA efforts may be hard to sustain."

Using a Cause Approach Rather Than a Blame Approach

To some extent, making people aware of their mistakes is necessary. This process can provide them with guidance by identifying their shortcomings. Leaving things at that, however, is not likely to serve the individual provider or the organization in the long run. Taking the approach that the quality improvement process should have an educational focus that reinforces the objective of changing behavior and improving employee performance will have more positive and far-reaching results. Identifying the cause of mistakes rather than assigning blame allows line supervisors to educate personnel. Often, many factors lead to the mistakes personnel make, and many of the reasons lie outside their control.

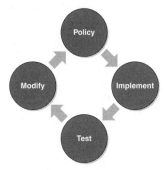

Quality Assurance Cycle

Source: Adapted from *A Leadership Guide to Quality Improvement for Emergency Medical Services Systems* (Eastham & Champion, 1997).

---

10 Reasons Employees Do Not Perform as Expected

1. Employers fail to communicate to employees why their work is important.
2. Employees do not receive timely feedback about their performance.
3. Supervisors fail to acknowledge individually how employees are affected by their work assignments.
4. The work environment contains physical or organizational performance obstacles.
5. Documentation sources are poorly designed, inaccessible, or nonexistent.
6. Employees lack the job aids necessary to guide correct performance.
7. Performance expectations are unclear or unstated.
8. Employees lack authority to do their jobs.
9. Doing the job correctly is punished or ignored.
10. Employees don't know how or have forgotten how to do their jobs.

Source: Boosting Employee Performance (Ginn, 2006).

Analyzing the Impact of Management on the Health of an Organization's Culture

In the 1980s, Professor Yoshikazu Tsuda, known for his work in quality management, published his observations on the health of an organization. He believed that "you can tell the state of health of a company by observing what and how topics are discussed in their management meetings" (as cited in Tribus, 1984). From his observations, it is clear that leaders who are more open to discussing problems and errors as well as successes regularly are the ones whose actions have the greatest positive effect on their organizations. This is important because all too often leaders are reluctant to discuss problems because they fear criticism and do not want to face blame. Perhaps this stems from their approach to the mistakes of their subordinates and tendency to assign blame versus finding root causes to fix the problem, or perhaps it comes from the organizational culture in which they served during their careers. Either way, approaching problems and situations with a reluctance to discuss how to address the root cause and an eye toward blame and punishment will have profound negative effects on personnel, morale, and the quality of service provided.

Organizational Health Is Reflected in the Management Meeting

- **A sick company**—Only things favorable to the speaker are reported
- **A not-so-sick company**—Unfavorable news is reported only in reply to a question. The source of the trouble is said to be not with the speaker
- **An ill company**—The speaker voluntarily gives bad news and an explanation. The management accepts the information
- **A weak company**—The board accepts the givens in the situation and tries to see what to do
- **A healthy company**—Speakers report good and bad news, give explanations and data freely, present an analysis of potentials to improve the system, review the givens in the situation. Board questions the givens and tries to develop creative alternatives

Source: Reducing Deming's 14 Points to Practice, Part II (Tribus, 1984).

Replace Punitive Consequences with Positive Reinforcement

Having disciplined professionals will go further than having employees who must be disciplined through punitive measures. Unfortunately, punitive measures often are linked too closely with quality assurance and improvement programs. Providing regular feedback on performance as part of the process is vital because if the only time providers hear about their performance is when they make mistakes, it will not be their fault that their perception is that QA = Discipline.

"Improved performance cannot take place unless workers feel comfortable that they can speak truthfully and are confident that their suggestions are taken seriously."

–James N. Eastham, Jr. and Howard R. Champion,
authors of *A Leadership Guide to Quality Improvement for Emergency Medical Services*

Leaders need to create opportunities for personnel to participate in the process and embrace mistakes as opportunities for growth and improvement. Leaders must get out of the mindset that making improvements is an admission of poor procedure and that, by extension, they too are in the wrong. Identifying a provider's strengths and reinforcing what the provider is doing well is as important to the process as pointing out shortcomings and providing the support to overcome problems. If providers sense that you see the good in what they do and not just their errors, they will be more inclined to listen and respond positively to your constructive criticism.

Understanding the Concept of Nonpunitive Close-Call Reporting

Nonpunitive close-call reporting is a concept based in part on the work of risk management pioneer Archand Zeller and his belief that "because man does not change, the kinds of errors he makes remains constant and the errors that he will make can be predicted from the errors that he has made" (as cited in Graham, 2004). This concept of predictability based on past performance provides the basis for addressing performance improvement through the use of individual mistakes.

To fully understand and appreciate the concept, let's take a brief look at the work of another risk management expert, H. W. Heinrich. Heinrich worked for an insurance company in the 1930s

> **"**Interjecting discipline into the QA process will encourage employees to provide false data out of fear of being disciplined.**"**
>
> –Gary Ludwig, Deputy Chief, Memphis (Tennessee) Fire Department

and studied tens of thousands of accident reports for both cause and blame. His work led to the theory that if you take a group of people doing the same or similar tasks (EMTs, paramedics, dispatchers, fire fighters, plumbers, electricians, etc.), many of the same mistakes that have occasionally ended up in tragedy were made hundreds of times by others with less severe outcomes. Historically, lessons have unfortunately been learned largely through the study of these tragedies. Your providers are part of your EMS agency, which is just one of many in your state and one of even more in the country. If we look across the board nationally, we will find that the mistakes that are being made are not isolated occurrences.

Let's take an example in which a BLS unit arrives on the scene of a motor vehicle collision and promptly cancels the ALS unit that is also dispatched because all occupants of the vehicles are out and walking around. A patient is transported to the closest hospital, which happens to also be a trauma center, and the emergency room staff discovers a closed head injury and questions why ALS was not treating the patient. An investigation is conducted, and it is determined that the crew did not properly assess the patient before canceling ALS. Action is taken with the individuals involved, and before long the incident is a distant memory. Now, what if we were to look further and discover that others made the same or a similar mistake numerous times in the past without significant consequence? Was the cause of this most recent mistake simply an error in judgment on the part of the EMTs involved, or could it be that overlooking or not identifying such behavior has become the norm?

To identify mistakes before they become mishaps or tragic events involving serious injury or death, honesty in reporting of the mistakes must occur. Using QA data for educational versus disciplinary purposes will help develop an environment in which people feel comfortable seeking out guidance when they make mistakes instead of hoping no one notices or, worse, actively covering up the mistake. By sharing mistakes in a nonpunitive and nonjudgmental way, we can learn from each other's mistakes so that the likelihood and frequency of negative occurrences is reduced.

Quality Assurance and Improvement

All too often in EMS agencies around the country and the world, quality assurance data are not collected or not used to their fullest potential, and their importance is not understood by leadership and providers alike. Some agencies have comprehensive, "model" QA-QI programs, and others that have none whatsoever; most fall somewhere in between. In their book *The Paramedic*, Chapleau et al. (2008) provide the guidance that "[q]uality improvement activities benefit all aspects of EMS, not just patient care. They provide systems with the ability to identify the best practices in all aspects of performance." When used in a meaningful way, the information gathered in the QA-QI process can have a profound impact on both individual and organizational performance improvement.

Language of Leadership

- **Standard**—A generalized goal that is an achievable model of excellence and is used to define expectations
- **Indicator**—An objective behavior or outcome that can be measured to determine compliance with a standard
- **Threshold**—An established level or percentage of acceptable compliance that indicates when further evaluation should be initiated
- **Trend**—A prevailing tendency

Let's look at an example in which it is discovered that a particular provider makes the same simple mistake on a regular basis. Identifying the issue of concern and then providing feedback and guidance will correct an ongoing behavior that might otherwise go unnoticed. Taking it a step further to an organizational view, suppose now we follow the same process and find that while most providers meet the agency threshold for overall patient care on most calls, the overall agency compliance with one or two key areas is below the threshold. We have now identified not only a trend but perhaps an agency norm as well. We can now develop a plan to address the issue in a positive way, such as through clinical counseling, increased focus, or including relative topics in upcoming continuing education activities. Adding trend identification and analysis to an existing quality assurance program need not be cumbersome. Much of the information is already being gathered; it just needs to be used to its fullest potential.

Leadership Through the Hollywood Lens

In the movie *Renaissance Man* (Marshall, 1994), the Army leadership at Fort McClane determines that a number of the recruits require remediation in comprehension and critical thinking to improve their overall performance. Bill Rago (played by Danny DeVito) is an unemployed advertising executive with a master's degree whom the unemployment office matches with the teaching position advertised at Fort McClane. Although Rago has the necessary credentials for the position, he has never taught before. As the movie progresses, he connects with his students when they show an interest in *Hamlet*. Although challenged in his approach by the drill instructor, Sergeant Cass (Gregory Hines), Rago successfully uses their interest in something he loves as a catalyst to reach them and help them overcome their shortcomings in comprehension and critical thinking. The experience also provides an opportunity for Rago to explore and overcome some of his own shortcomings and realize the importance of listening to others and being supportive.

The people in our organizations look to us as EMS leaders for guidance and support. They expect us to take their concerns seriously and often do not realize that what is of vital importance to them may not be as pertinent to us because their concern is simply one of many on our plates. Additionally, from our perspective, and often in reality as well, their issues may be of lower priority to the organization overall. Taking concerns seriously, no matter how small they may seem to us, has an impact that goes far beyond the particular issue. It represents the relationship between leaders and their people. Taking each of their concerns seriously fosters a connection, builds trust, and shows employees that their leader cares about issues that their followers find important. So, even if you cannot get to the "fix" for their issue right away, at least acknowledge that it exists and set a time frame (and stick to it) within which you can help them. By recognizing their concerns as important, your people will know that they can come to you, and you will reap the intrinsic reward of knowing that you took the time to listen.

Critical Thinking Skills

The complexities and ever-changing world of EMS demand that its providers and especially its leaders attain a higher level of thinking. Historically, passing certification and licensing exams involved much memorization and total recall of facts associated with the base of clinical knowledge required of the various levels of EMS providers. However, once in the field, the ability to perform and improve requires an understanding of why procedures are done a certain way and how to adapt to surprising situations that don't occur in the classroom. The ability to conceptualize situations, make decisions to solve problems, and address the needs of our patients, subordinates, and organizations is a vital skill at every level of EMS.

> **The Six Rs of Critical Thinking**
>
> - Remembering
> - Repeating
> - Reasoning
> - Recognizing
> - Relating
> - Reflecting
>
> *Source: Foundations of Education: An EMS Approach* (Cason, 2006).

Performance Evaluations as a Tool for Performance Improvement and Career Development

Whether career or volunteer, EMS professionals find their involvement in the industry to be meaningful for any number of intrinsic and extrinsic reasons. Therefore, it is realistic to believe that most, if not all, EMS providers have a desire to improve their performance.

If your performance evaluations are nothing more than another task with a deadline, then you and your organization may be neglecting a valuable performance improvement tool. Telling someone at the end of the year what his or her strengths and weaknesses are has merit, but keeping that person informed and involved in professional growth and development throughout the year has even greater potential for performance improvement. For example, if you wait until the person's annual review to identify a weakness in performance that existed all year, you have just taken away months of opportunities for him or her to work on it. Meeting with your people early and often will create more opportunities for involvement in their own improvement as well as for you to guide them and grow as a leader.

Using the performance evaluation as a platform for ongoing performance improvement need not require that you change the form or the deadline. All it requires is a different, more proactive and interactive approach. Scheduling time early in the year to review the previous evaluation and discuss strengths, weaknesses, and goals with personnel is a great place to start. Together, you and each subordinate can develop an action plan that serves as a roadmap for them to use in achieving their goals and improving on their weaknesses. Based on the needs of the individual, provide the necessary support throughout the year that will give him or her the best chance at success, and schedule at least one more meeting at the midpoint between your initial counseling session and the due date for the evaluations.

For the midpoint counseling session, encourage subordinates to bring "bragging points" of their accomplishments as well as a list of any unresolved or newly discovered issues or concerns affecting their performance. At the midpoint session, you and your subordinates can discuss

> **"**Vocational theorists and psychological research tell us that people want to do their best in tasks that are meaningful to them.**"**
>
> –Hendrie Weisinger, author of *The Power of Positive Criticism*

Leadership Lessons from History

In 2005, "Hurricane Katrina made landfall, destroying both the Gulf Coast and the reputation of the Federal Emergency Management Agency (FEMA) when it failed to carry out its mission of coordinating disaster relief" (Magnuson, 2007). Since then, the new director, R. David Paulson, has led the agency in learning from its mistakes and using them as a catalyst for changing the way FEMA approaches disaster preparedness and response. According to its website, "FEMA has learned many lessons from its experiences during Hurricane Katrina and has implemented numerous changes in order to improve its operations. Furthermore, post-Katrina legislation has enabled the Agency to create a vision for a 'New FEMA'" (FEMA, 2007).

If you consider the feedback and criticism that FEMA received post-Katrina, they clearly received the good, the bad, and the ugly from all angles. FEMA was a piñata for all to take swings at—many warranted, many not. The new leadership, however, appears to have taken the 360° input seriously and used it for what has already shown to be improved performance in response to many of the disasters that have occurred since 2005.

progress and adjust the goals and plans to reach them accordingly so that they can spend the next few months working to further refine their performance.

As the deadline for completion of the evaluations approaches, instruct your subordinates to develop a final sheet of bragging points as well as a draft of what they believe their evaluation should look like based on their performance over the course of the year. To help prepare them for this assignment, it is important that you provide them with a blank evaluation form and copies of their last evaluation or two at the first meeting and ensure that they have what they need to get the job done in the final weeks before the evaluations are due.

When you collect and review their input, you will find that having followed an ongoing process throughout the year has better prepared you for your task of completing and submitting performance evaluations and simultaneously has helped your staff and the organization improve.

The 360° Feedback Concept

The 360° evaluation and feedback process uses the input of superiors, peers, and subordinates in the evaluation of an individual. This multirater concept has grown in popularity and use, particularly in the area of leadership development. In its simplest form, the way a 360° evaluation process works is that participants are selected along with their subordinates, peers, and superiors who complete an evaluation of the participant. The feedback is gathered and compiled into a final product that is then shared with the participant. In discussing this process, it is important to note

"What your boss, your peers, and your subordinates really think of you may sting, but facing the truth can also make you a better manager.**"**

–Cynthia D. McCauley and Ellen Van Velsor, coeditors of the *Handbook of Leadership Development*

> **"***Don't mind criticism. If it is untrue, disregard it; if unfair, keep from irritation; if it is ignorant, smile; if it is justified, it is not criticism.***"**
>
> –Anonymous, *The Starbucks Experience* by Joseph A. Michelli

that "when a methodology becomes as popular as 360-degree feedback has become, interest in best practices runs high as do concerns about misuse" (McCauley & Van Velsor, 2004). Therefore, although the person being evaluated benefits by receiving a variety of perspectives, there is the challenge of ensuring that the feedback is genuine and not tainted by biased or inappropriate commentary. Thus, raters should be cautioned not to simply point out weaknesses but to discuss strengths as well and to do so in a manner consistent with how they would like to receive similar positive reinforcement and constructive criticism.

Positive Criticism

When providing feedback, particularly if a person did not perform as desired, as expected, or in keeping with his or her potential, it is important that the individual's self-esteem not be unduly harmed in the process. The old saying that "sticks and stones may break my bones, but names will never hurt me" does not necessarily hold true. In fact, words can do harm, particularly when they come from someone in authority. "[I]ndeed criticism and self-esteem have a long and intimate relationship, and it is the closeness of the relationship that gives criticism the power to affect self-esteem for better or for worse" (Weisinger, 2000). When you are providing constructive criticism, it is important to be specific and stick to the facts while avoiding the interjection of your feelings. It is important that the person knows you are discussing the actual situation and not just the effect his or her behavior had on you and your feelings. Additionally, just as with discipline, it is important that you wait and prepare your thoughts without the impact of any emotional response you may have initially had to the person's mistake. Remember that approaching someone with a concern about behavior or performance is difficult for everyone involved. Taking the time to properly prepare yourself and your subordinate for the encounter will go a long way toward ensuring a meaningful outcome.

You Are the EMS Leader

You have a number of EMS supervisors who are responsible for conducting quality assurance reviews for the providers that report to them. As is sometimes the case with life and work, one or more of them will on occasion miss a deadline, but one specific member of your staff consistently does not meet the deadline and sometimes doesn't complete the work at all.

1. What are your concerns with this behavior and how would you approach the issue?

2. As you prepare to meet with the person about the issue, can you think of any contributing factors that might mitigate the behavior? Explain your reasons for each.

3. When you meet with the person, she advises you that she simply does not have sufficient time to perform the performance evaluation. Given that all the other supervisory personnel at her level are scheduled the same amount of hours and that the others, with the few exceptions already noted, consistently meet the mark, how would you proceed?

4. What impact do you believe this ongoing issue has had on the performance of the others involved?

5. What impact could letting the behavior continue have?

Wrap-Up

Chapter Summary

Everyone wants to succeed and improve their performance in the areas that are important to them. Thus EMS leaders are in a unique position to facilitate or hinder such improvement in their people and themselves. Recognizing the strengths and weaknesses of yourself and your people and taking a proactive and creative approach to addressing them will provide lasting value to everyone involved. Personnel at every level of an organization face challenges in their performance. As a leader in EMS, it is your responsibility to provide the structure, experience, guidance, and focus that foster positive subordinate development. Taking the time to approach mistakes and other situations involving criticism in a positive way will change you and your people into creative, active thinkers who use every opportunity, both positive and negative, to create improvement. Furthermore, understanding not only that allowed behavior will become the standard in your organization and recognizing the importance of maintaining high standards and taking swift action to address behavior will help you establish a professional atmosphere. Quality and performance improvement should be embraced as an ongoing process within the organizational culture.

Why Their Views Matter: About the Authors Cited in the Chapter

John M. Becknell is the publisher of the *EMS Best Practices* newsletter. He has been in EMS for more than 25 years and is the author of the book *Medic Life: Creating Success in EMS.*

Angel Clark Burba is associate professor and EMS Program Director at Howard Community College in Columbia, Maryland. She is a volunteer paramedic with the Boonsboro Volunteer Rescue Service in Boonsboro, Maryland. She is coauthor of the text *The Paramedic* and served as president of the National Association of EMS Educators.

Debra Cason is an associate professor and the program director for emergency medicine education at the University of Texas Southwestern medical center and is the editor of *Foundations of Education: An EMS Approach.*

Howard R. Champion was one of two coprincipal investigators of *A Leadership Guide to Quality Improvement for Emergency Medical Services (EMS) Systems.* He is a visiting scholar at the National Study Center for Trauma and EMS at the University of Maryland at Baltimore and professor of surgery and chief of trauma at the Uniformed Services University of the Health Sciences at Bethesda, Maryland.

Will Chapleau is manager of the ATLS Program with the American College of Surgeons in Chicago and coauthor of the text *The Paramedic.*

Calvin Coolidge served as president of the United States from 1923 to 1929. He had been mayor of Northampton, Massachusetts, and a state representative and senator before becoming the 30th president. He was considered frugal by many and effectively cut taxes for people earning less than $10,000 per year. Additionally, he raised ethical standards in Washington and was considered to honest, shrewd, and modest. Professor John McGinnis of Northeastern University believed he used these traits to provide a model for the kind of leader a republic needs.

W. Edwards Deming received a BS degree from the University of Wyoming at Laramie. He received an MS degree from the University of Colorado and a PhD from Yale University. He was a professor, lecturer, and consultant who made significant contributions to both Japanese and American industrial quality and production.

James N. Eastham, Jr. was one of two coprincipal investigators of *A Leadership Guide to Quality Improvement for Emergency Medical Services (EMS) Systems.* He is an associate professor of emergency health services at the University of Maryland, Baltimore County.

Charles Ginn is director of performance improvement for Administaff. He is the author of a series of articles focusing on employee performance, including *Boosting Employee Performance: 10 Reasons Employees Do Not Perform as Expected* and *Employees Remember Informal Training Best.*

Gordon Graham has more than 30 years of experience in law enforcement. He is also a practicing attorney. He graduated from the University of Southern California with an MS degree in safety and systems management. Graham is widely known for providing his knowledge to both public- and private-sector organizations in the area of organizational and operational risk management, civil liability, professionalism, ethical decision making, and other related topics. He is a prolific public speaker, having given upward of 3,000 presentations to a variety of audiences in the last decade.

Gary Ludwig is Deputy Fire Chief of the Memphis (Tennessee) Fire Department. He has more than 30 years of experience in fire and EMS, including 25 years with the city of St. Louis, where he retired at the rank of chief paramedic. He also served as president of the IAFC EMS Section. He regularly writes on the topic of leadership for national trade magazines and shares his insights at conferences throughout the United States.

Cynthia D. McCauley is a senior fellow at the Center for Creative Leadership. She is published in numerous professional journals, including the *Journal of Management*. She is coeditor of the *Handbook of Leadership Development*.

David Page is on the faculty of the Emergency Health Services Department at Inner Hills Community College in Minnesota and is a paramedic with Allina Medical Transportation in St. Paul, Minnesota. He is coauthor of the text *The Paramedic*.

Peter T. Pons is an emergency physician in Denver, Colorado, and coauthor of the text *The Paramedic*.

Myron Tribus served as director of the Center for Advanced Engineering Study at the Massachusetts Institute of Technology and as chairman of the Technology Task Force at the National Society of Professional Engineers in Alexandria, Virginia.

Yoshikazu Tsuda a professor at St. Paul's University in Tokyo, is a member of the Deming Prize Committee and a lecturer for the Japanese Union of Scientists and Engineers and the Association of Overseas Technical Scholars. He has served as a busy consultant to numerous companies in Japan, Bulgaria, the United States, and Belgium. His specialty is quality management.

Ellen Van Velsor is a senior research scientist and a research and development director at the Center for Creative Leadership. She is coauthor of *Breaking the Glass Ceiling: Can Women Reach the Top of America's Largest Corporations?* and is the coeditor of the *Handbook of Leadership Development*.

Hendrie Weisinger is a licensed psychologist who has made hundreds of appearances on television and news programs. He is considered an authority on emotional intelligence and anger management and is the author of *The Power of Positive Criticism*.

Chapter 9

Leading Change

❚❚ This 'telephone' has too many shortcomings to be seriously considered as a means of communication. The device is inherently of no value to us. **❚❚**

—Western Union Internal Memo, 1876

Introduction

Leadership in general and leading an EMS organization in particular is challenging. Leading change is perhaps the most difficult of all leadership responsibilities. In his book, *Leading Change*, Harvard Business School professor John P. Kotter tells us that "[l]eadership defines what the future should look like, aligns people with that vision, and inspires them to make it happen despite the obstacles." Sometimes those obstacles are things like cost, and at other times they are things like the belief that change is not possible, needed, or feasible. Change is nothing new to EMS. Every few years we all learn a new way to do CPR. New medications and equipment are developed that change the way both ALS and BLS personnel approach the same medical and trauma calls. Suddenly, calls that they have handled for years require different medications, different equipment, and different procedures. To make change possible, leaders not only must set the vision, but they must also understand the change process and provide guidance to their people and their organization.

Understanding the Change Process

When seeking to change how an EMS organization approaches work that it has been doing in the same way for a long time, those leading change must grasp the cycle of change. According to psychologist Kurt Lewin (as cited in Yukl, 2006), "the change process can be divided into three phases: unfreezing, changing, and refreezing." In the unfreezing phase, leaders and in turn followers realize that the old methods are not working or are not as efficient or effective as they could be. In the changing phase, new approaches are sought. Then in the refreezing phase, these new approaches are implemented and become established. What needs to take place next

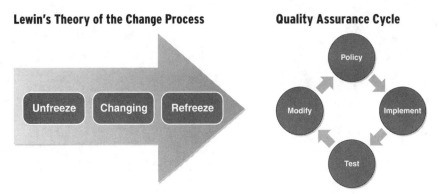

Source: Adapted from *Leadership in Organizations* (Yukl, 2006). and *A Leadership Guide to Quality Improvement for Emergency Medical Services Systems* (Eastham & Champion, 1997)

is open-minded and unbiased monitoring of the impact of the changes to be sure they meet the desired goals, or at least that they improve what the organization and its people are doing. Applying the Deming PDCA cycle discussed in Chapter 8 is one way to monitor the change process and even the specific elements within the process. The important thing is that the EMS leader embarking on a mission of change understands the process, its impact on people, and the need to monitor progress and apply flexibility to achieve the desired results.

Recognizing and Responding to the Need for Change

Michael Beer, in a chapter about leading, learning, and learning to lead in the *Leader's Change Handbook* (Conger, Spreitzer, & Lawler, 1999), writes about "the importance of creating dissatisfaction with the status quo, changing behavior by focusing on the task, fostering learning by doing instead of classroom training or other human resource programs, a clear model or vision of the future state, and the importance of using the change process to develop or replace key actors in the organization." For change to occur, Beer tells us that someone with a vision must step forward and put forth that vision, or that something significant must happen that serves as a catalyst for those in power to break with the status quo.

All too often, people in leadership positions put too much stock in creating a catchy theme as the primary means of generating buy-in for the changes they seek to implement. While there may be some benefit in themes, as Eric Yaverbaum (2006) puts it in his book *Leadership Secrets of the World's Most Successful CEOs*, "business cannot rely on clichés—old encapsulated thought patterns—or trendy catchphrases, which are nothing more than new encapsulated thought patterns." By encapsulating an idea or vision, leaders tend to limit options and thereby diminish the likelihood that attempts at comprehensive organizational change will be effective. If we think about our practice of prehospital patient assessment, we are encouraged to ask open-ended questions of our patients to allow them to describe their situations. We are also taught to consider multiple causes for a patient's symptoms, thereby minimizing the likelihood of missing one thing because we are focusing on another. As EMS leaders we can use these same skills that we have developed as providers and apply them in a variety of ways to facilitate change.

The saying goes that "you can't teach an old dog new tricks," but the problem often rests not in the dogs but in how the tricks are presented and taught. Leaders who are able to put aside whatever strong feelings many may have about how a situation should be handled, and take the time to build a team and reach consensus, will be more likely to have followers who provide honest feedback and constructive criticism. Including your colleagues in each stage of the process will give you the greatest chance of a successful organizational change.

Leadership Lessons from History

Former Soviet Union President Mikhail Gorbachev believed that Soviet society needed to change because it suppressed the human being. Many of his countrymen considered his philosophy unorthodox. According to Gorbachev (as cited in Lowe, 2006), "the more I saw the more I analyzed and thought about what was happening—I knew that something was wrong and really not working." At the core of Gorbachev's approach was a belief that a successful leader should implement projects that benefit the majority, and that change should not be implemented solely for the benefit of an individual. In order to achieve his sweeping reformation of his society, Gorbachev realized that it was important to build trusting relationships with world leaders, including former enemies like the United States. Gorbachev was recognized for his work in changing the Soviet Union and his contributions to ending the Cold War with a Nobel Peace Prize. He is considered by many to be one of the 20th century's most pivotal world leaders.

Implementing Change

When you are implementing change, it is important that there is a legitimate need or purpose for the change. Buying a new piece of equipment, for example, just because it is the latest model is not sufficient justification, particularly if the new equipment will require retraining or a change in how you operate. The benefits of the change must be weighed against the benefits of continuing the usual operating procedures. The negatives of both the change and the status quo also must be factored in. Above all, there must be a vision of where this change will take the organization as a whole.

Creating a vision is not easy, but, when effectively established, it can play a critical role in making sure that everyone is moving in the same direction. It is important that leaders develop a vision regarding change and that they strive to align constituencies to that vision by educating, enlightening, and empowering their people. Change is an arduous task that should not be taken lightly. Implementing new procedures requires expertise and will affect perceptions, norms, and work behaviors. Therefore, leading and implementing change must be well thought out, flexible, and begin with the end in mind.

Resistance to Change

When people in an organization see changes only in relation to how their own position is affected, they will likely resist those changes because without seeing the big picture, they will be unable to envision the potential positive impact on the overall organization. Therefore, when preparing to implement change it is important that leaders take the time to listen and to empathize with their

"When each person defends a personalized and therefore partial view of systemic challenges, then leadership is rendered ineffective."

–Jay A. Conger, Gretchen M. Spreitzer, and Edward E. Lawler III, authors of *The Leader's Change Handbook*

Leadership Through the Hollywood Lens

The movie *Sister Act* (Ardolino, 1992) is about a professional lounge singer named Deloris Van Cartier (played by Whoopi Goldberg) who witnesses a mob-related murder. The traditional Mother Superior of a convent (Maggie Smith) is engaged by Los Angeles Police Lieutenant Eddie Souther (Bill Nunn) to hide and protect Deloris until she testifies at the murder trial. The Mother Superior expresses her concerns about the unusual situation to Monsignor O'Hara (Joseph Maher) but is convinced by him to take on the challenge and responsibility of protecting Deloris from harm. As part of her plan to make Deloris more inconspicuous, the Mother Superior disguises her as Sister Mary Clarence, a nun from a progressive convent in Nevada. When "Sister Mary Clarence" has difficulty fitting into the very conservative and traditional convent, the Reverend Mother assigns her to sing in the choir.

Eager to improve, the members of the choir ask Deloris for her professional help. Initially, the leader of the choir, Sister Mary Lazarus (Mary Wickes), balks at Deloris' changes and is somewhat insulted by what she refers to as a "mutiny" against her by the members of the choir. Deloris immediately recognizes Sister Mary Lazarus' concerns and tactfully enlists her support in guiding the choir by tapping into her sense of duty and regimented ways. Together they lead the choir's journey of change and transformation. Within a short time, Deloris's impact on the choir is profoundly evident in their performance at Sunday services, but the Mother Superior is not pleased with the drastic change from a traditional to a more contemporary and "worldly" approach.

After the church service, Monsignor O'Hara, who is pleased with the changes that have taken place so far and pleased that the sisters have a desire to do more, overhears the Mother Superior reprimanding Sister Mary Clarence. Monsignor O'Hara seizes the opportunity to tactfully influence the Mother Superior. His approach is to intervene and credit her with the vision and the benefits of the changes in the choir. Seeing this, Deloris uses the opportunity to suggest even more changes in the form of an expanded role for the sisters in the community. Together, Sister Mary Clarence and Monsignor O'Hara lead the change that has been long overdue.

When Deloris was introduced to the convent, its routine was disrupted. Her presence begins to change their traditional ways by opening up possibilities for them to do more both inside the convent and in the community. Prompted by their recent successes, the Pope visits their church, which further validates their work. When Deloris leaves, the sisters' confidence is high, and the changes begin to take hold. In the end, Deloris returns to civilian life, and the Mother Superior and sisters of Saint Catherine's Convent are left with significant positive changes to what they do and how they do it. Most importantly, when they part ways with Sister Mary Clarence, they are prepared to sustain the improvements to their way of life. The film is a classic example of Lewin's (1951) theory of the change process in action.

people. Not all fears and objections will be put to rest, but a better understanding will be established for both leaders and followers. Each will need to adjust his or her approach somewhat. By collaborating, the difficult effects of the process will be minimized, and a deeper trust between colleagues will develop.

Overcoming the Organizational Comfort Zone

When we look at organizations and the people that make them up, we must realize that "established organizations manifest organizational learning that has occurred within a particular paradigm, or way of doing things, that has sufficed in earlier environments" (Conger et al., 1999). To me, this was the old "if it's not broken, don't fix it" approach to leadership. However, simply functioning with past procedures is no guarantee that they will continue to work as the environment outside the organization changes. There is a phrase I have heard quoted over the years: "If we keep doing what we're doing, we'll keep being what we've been." The source of the original quote is unknown, but it supports the position that radical organizational change cannot be accomplished without using collaboration and shared leadership.

> **Common Reasons People Resist Change**
>
> 1. Lack of trust
> 2. Belief that change is not necessary
> 3. Belief that change is not feasible
> 4. Economic threats
> 5. Relative high cost
> 6. Fear of personal failure
> 7. Loss of status and power
> 8. Threat to values and ideals
> 9. Resentment of interference
>
> *Source: Leadership in Organizations* (Yukl, 2006).

Often, leaders do work hard enough to convince their colleagues that change is necessary and therefore lack a vital part of value-based leadership—teamwork. By not realizing the importance of collaboration from the members or stakeholders in an organization, leaders sabotage their own vision and their efforts to facilitate change.

"By far, the biggest mistake people make when trying to change organizations is to plunge ahead without establishing enough sense of urgency in fellow managers and employees."

–John P. Kotter, author of *Leading Change*

You Are the EMS Leader

As is the case with many volunteer EMS agencies across the country, the membership is empowered to enact and amend the bylaws by which they are governed and must operate. For readers who have served on bylaws committees or otherwise gone through the process of amending bylaws, there need be no further explanation. For those who have not yet had the opportunity, perhaps this case study will provide some insight.

Leaders and members of your agency have recognized and identified the need for changes to your bylaws, and as an EMS leader you were appointed to the committee to review and recommend changes to bylaws that have been in existence for more than 30 years. The latest significant modification took place 10 years ago. You and your fellow committee members hold a number of meetings over a period of 2 months, and between the meetings you all actively seek input from a cross section of the membership. Members and past leaders of the organization also volunteer their insights, ideas, and concerns.

The final product is presented over two membership meetings, and it is discussed and debated at length. A vote is taken and all but a handful of the dozens of revisions you and the committee worked so hard to put together are approved. You struggled through the process and are largely pleased with the results.

A few weeks later, a member mentions one of the proposed changes that had not been approved and states that, although it was rejected, the fact that it was even brought up has cut deep wounds that have permanently damaged and divided the organization.

1. *What is your initial reaction to these concerns?*

2. *In general, how would you approach the matter and what advice might you have for this individual about overcoming these feelings?*

3. *Given the scenario and that you and the rest of the committee tried to approach the process with an open mind and to include everyone's ideas for the membership as a whole to vote on, do you believe their feelings are more personal because they disagreed with the proposed change?*

4. *Depending on your belief about the member's bias or objective view, discuss some of the specific concerns you have about the potential for long-lasting damage to the organization.*

5. *Would you approach the member's concerns differently if you were personally in favor of the proposed change than if you believed that the proposed change was not needed? Why or why not?*

6. *What lessons about change and the change process can you as an EMS leader take away from a situation involving change in which people have very strong views on both sides of the issue?*

Wrap-Up

Chapter Summary

Most leaders, especially the successful ones, have a vision for change, but sometimes lack sufficient understanding of the concepts necessary to implement their ideas. Because of this, leaders are often unable to bring about lasting organizational change. Understanding the process of change, how it occurs, and the possibility of resistance to the change will serve the EMS leader well. EMS providers and leaders, by the nature of the profession, have become skilled at quickly analyzing situations and forming their own opinions and plans about how they should be handled. Building a consensus and including the input of others before, during, and after change takes place will allow the EMS leader not only to achieve positive results but to sustain them as well.

Why Their Views Matter: About the Authors Cited in the Chapter

Jay A. Conger is a professor of business administration at the Marshall School of Business at the University of Southern California. He is executive director of the Leadership Institute and coeditor of *The Leader's Change Handbook*.

W. Edwards Deming received a BS degree from the University of Wyoming at Laramie. He received an MS degree from the University of Colorado and a PhD from Yale University. He was a professor, lecturer, and consultant who made significant contributions to both Japanese and American industrial quality and production.

Mikhail Gorbachev was listed as one of *Time Magazine's* 100 Leaders and Revolutionaries. He was the president of the Soviet Union and made great strides in Soviet government reform. His collaboration with U.S. President Ronald Reagan contributed to the end of the Cold War. In 1990 he was awarded the Nobel Peace Prize. Since his resignation, he has remained active in world affairs and in 1992 founded the Gorbachev Foundation.

John P. Kotter is the Konosuke Matsushita Professor of Leadership Emeritus at Harvard Business School. He is the author of a number of books, including seven best-sellers. Among his books are *Leading Change, The Heart of Change*, and *The Heart of Change Field Guide.*

Edward E. Lawler III is the founder and director of the Center for Effective Organizations and is a professor of business administration at the University of Southern California. He has been recognized by *Business Week* for his expertise in management and is coeditor of *The Leader's Change Handbook*.

Gretchen M. Spreitzer is an assistant professor of business administration at the University of Southern California. She is widely recognized for her work on empowerment and leadership. She is coeditor of *The Leader's Change Handbook*.

Eric Yaverbaum is president of the New York City–based public relations firm Jericho. He has appeared on the *Today Show* and *Larry King Live.* He is the author of a number of books, including *I'll Get Back to You* and *Leadership Secrets of the World's Most Successful CEOs.*

Gary Yukl holds a PhD from the University of California at Berkeley and is a professor at the State University of New York at Albany. He is the author of the text *Leadership in Organizations,* which focuses on effective leadership in organizations through both theory and practice. His leadership provides us an insightful look at the use of power and how its components can influence the behavior of subordinates and peers.

Chapter 10

Team Building

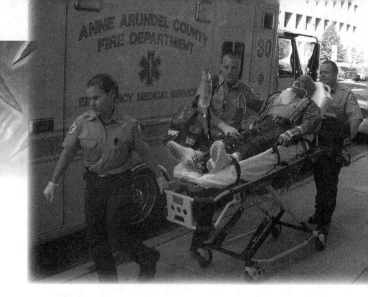

> **❝**It's surprising how much you can accomplish if you don't care who gets the credit.**❞**

—Abraham Lincoln

Introduction

Teamwork in EMS is essential to providing safe and efficient patient care. Even for the greatest of leaders, it can be difficult to create a cohesive environment in which everyone makes the team their first priority. The key to unlocking the collective power of a team lies in the leader's understanding that, as Charlie Weiss, head coach of the Notre Dame football team, writes in his book *No Excuses* (Weiss & Carucci, 2006), "once you can get people to not think selfishly, to suppress their egos and to focus on how they can make the team better, success can be achieved."

In this chapter, we will explore the concept of teams and teamwork as well as continue to examine the importance of trust and communication. We will also consider the positives and negatives of the impact of conflict on both team cohesion and development. Additionally, we will look at the different ways to develop and sustain a team. EMS professionals are trained to think and act independently or to work in smaller teams, such as with a partner. Thus, having a better understanding of how to analyze, develop, and lead teams (both small and large) is invaluable to the development of the EMS leader.

Teams in EMS

In EMS, we find both interacting and co-acting teams. The simplest example of the interacting team in EMS is the partnership between two EMTs or paramedics. If we look closely at EMS, we see we have many co-acting teams. For example, field crews work with the support of the organization's mechanics. This collaborative relationship is considered a co-acting team. Separately, the mechanics and the field crews are interacting teams, but, when they work together to provide safe, quality patient care, they become a larger co-acting

Language of Leadership

- **Team**—A small task group in which members have a common purpose, interdependent roles, and complementary skills
- **Interacting Team**—A team, such as in basketball or soccer, within which members have interdependent roles
- **Co-acting Team**—A team, such as in bowling or wrestling, in which members work independently for an overall common purpose

team. Each EMS agency uses a combination of interactive and coactive teams to most efficiently provide care.

In addition to the internal team relationships of EMS organizations, there are external team relationships with similar and dissimilar dynamics. For example, police and EMS are essentially co-acting teams with the overall common goal of providing for public safety. However, when police and EMS personnel work together at the scene of an emergency, the personnel become a pro tem interactive team. After addressing the situation, they will then return to being coactive until the next emergency.

Understanding the dynamics of teams and how they work both inside and outside the EMS agency is important to the EMS leader because it is the leader's understanding and ability to adapt to the dynamic nature of teams in the emergency services environment that facilitates or inhibits the team's ability to perform to its fullest potential.

The Importance of Trust and Communication

Trust is at the center of every successful team relationship. To build trust, team members must not only communicate with each other, but must feel comfortable enough to communicate candidly and freely. Communication and trust are inextricably linked, and they are central to any discussion of team building. Linda Diamond and Harriet Diamond, authors of *Teambuilding That Gets Results* (2007), put it like this: "If items are slipping through the cracks, and your team has more excuses than results, all communication was a waste of time." With their views in mind, it is clear that shortcomings, in either or both of these areas, can be fatal to any team or group environment if not identified and addressed quickly.

It has been said that actions speak louder than words. Thus, action is communication in deeds and gestures that, if genuine, will build and maintain the trust required for a team to remain effective. A leader must take responsibility for his or her team's mistakes and publicly praise the team for its successes. This foresight will demonstrate the leader's commitment to maintaining and improving the team's environment. Open and honest dialogue will result in a more collaborative and respectful group setting. This dialogue can be established by communicating that individual, and even collective, vulnerability will be accepted without judgment.

Communication is not just telling the *what* but also telling the *why* behind it. This concept is not new to successful teams. Vince Lombardi, Jr. (2005), author of *The Lombardi Rules*, reminds us that "[i]f your people know the larger goals, and see the connection between their daily individual effort and achieving these goals, their motivation—and their ability to succeed—will be greatly enhanced." When people understand both what is going on and why, that increased comprehension and motivation will enhance their knowledge and ability to contribute in a more meaningful way while providing them with a sense of connection and inclusion in the process and the project.

> **"**It is important to acknowledge that language and attitude can either facilitate or inhibit an open discussion.**"**
>
> –Frank LaFasto and Carl Larson, coauthors of *When Teams Work Best*

> **"**The most important action that a leader must take to encourage the building of trust on a team is to demonstrate vulnerability first.**"**
>
> –Patrick Lencioni, author of *The Five Dysfunctions of a Team*

> **"**I try always to tell my players why we're doing certain drills, practicing shorter or longer, and why we work on certain things on certain days. I'm the head coach, yes and I suppose I could just bark it out and they'd do it, but by letting them in on my thought process, I am including them in what we're trying to accomplish.**"**
>
> –Herman Edwards, Head Coach, Kansas City Chiefs

Team Building

In the team environment, relationships are not just between two individuals, but involve a more complicated group dynamic. Whether selecting one specific model or developing your own organization-specific hybrid approach, it is important to remember that in building teams and resolving individual differences, the discussions should be narrowed to one issue at a time. To best neutralize defensiveness, each perspective should be given its due attention before reaching the final verdict. Additionally, a decision should be made before a related situation occurs that the team must then face together. Each member should, as part of the commitment to the team, endeavor to change at least one behavior in a manner that is beneficial to the team and its objectives. Each success and failure should be recorded to allow for follow-up analysis and to be used as the basis of tracking progress.

Although these ideas are important components to any teambuilding strategy, there are many approaches that incorporate them as well as have a specific focus. For example, Diamond and Diamond (2007) put forth a seven-step approach, whereas LaFasto and Larson (2001) use what they refer to as a CONNECT model to illustrate their belief that teams work best when members commit to the

---

The Developmental Feedback Model

1. State the problem
2. State job-related consequences and concerns
3. Probe to identify the cause of the problem
4. Listen actively
5. Ask team members for solution suggestions
6. Develop a concise plan with the team members
7. Summarize and set a time for follow-up

Source: Adapted from *Teambuilding That Gets Results* (Diamond & Diamond, 2007).

Leadership Lessons from History

In the second game of the 2000 NFL season, New England Patriots quarterback Drew Bledsoe was seriously injured. In comes Tom Brady, then a back-up with limited NFL game time experience. As coauthor of the book, *No Excuses* (2006), then offensive coordinator Charlie Weiss wrote,

I wasn't worried about whether he was ready to play. That was who was going in next, right? That was the way we thought as a team. We never worried whether a guy was ready. Whoever was next, that was who was next. His job was to be ready.

While Bledsoe was out recuperating from his injury, the dynamics and even the chemistry of the team changed. When he returned, the decision was made to allow Tom Brady to finish out the season and the postseason as the starter. While some may have allowed their egos to get in the way in such a situation, Drew Bledsoe was the consummate professional and a man of character. Having been part of, and in fact the center of, the team for many years, he not only understood the importance of the team-over-individual approach of the Patriots, but he had taught it to many members of the team and truly believed in it.

As the season continued, Bledsoe became somewhat of a mentor for Brady. At the same time, Bledsoe made sure he was ready to fill in for Brady, should he be needed. And, in the AFC championship game, Tom Brady was injured seriously enough to be removed from the game. With the roles reversed, Bledsoe was ready to fill in for Brady. Both Bledsoe and Brady's abilities to place their team as first priority reinforce the Patriots' approach to success. It also proves that, when understood and executed by every individual, this mentality truly results in triumph, and, for the Patriots, the season ended with the team's first-ever Super Bowl victory.

required relationships in a way that optimizes the safety and comfort zones of everyone involved. By starting with a mutual commitment that fosters cooperation and shared ownership, the team maintains a safe environment while working together to share ideas, understand each others' perspectives, and resolve differences. Whichever approach is taken, cooperation, consistency, and follow-through are vitally important.

Facilitators and Inhibitors

In building and maintaining teams, there will often be facilitators and inhibitors whose messages contribute to the success or failure of a group. Both types of leaders push their respective agendas in large part through the communication of their message. In these positive and negative examples, it is often more about how they say something that brings their message to life. For example, in their book *When Teams Work Best* (2001), Frank LaFasto and Carl Larson give us the phrases "help me understand why you feel the way you do" and "you have no right to feel that way" to illustrate facilitative and inhibitive communication, respectively.

The person in either of these leadership roles needs not have an official title to communicate the message. In any given "us versus them" encounter, the effectiveness of the leader's message is often linked to the level of trust

---

The CONNECT Model

- **C**ommit to the relationship
- **O**ptimize Safety
- **N**arrow the discussion to one issue
- **N**eutralize defensiveness
- **E**xplain and echo each perspective
- **C**hange one behavior each
- **T**rack it

Source: *When Teams Work Best* (LaFasto and Larson, 2001).

Language of Leadership

- **Cohesiveness**—The act or state of sticking together tightly
- **Collaboration**—To work jointly with others
- **Consensus**—Group solidarity in sentiment or belief

Leadership Through the Hollywood Lens

When Danny Ocean (played by George Clooney) is released on probation, he has a vision: to commit a sophisticated robbery from a vault holding the cash of three Las Vegas casinos on a fight night. With this vision in mind, he begins to build the *Ocean's Eleven* (Soderbergh, 2001) team. Given the potential financial gain, Ocean clearly has an extrinsic motivator, but he is also intrinsically motivated by both the challenge of the robbery and the opportunity to wreak havoc on the casino's owner, Terry Benedict (Andy Garcia), who is dating Ocean's ex-wife, Tess (Julia Roberts).

Ocean puts together his team by first selecting a right-hand man, Rusty Ryan (Brad Pitt), who in turn helps him with the initial plan and selection of the rest of the team members. The strength of their team rests not only in their individual talents and motivations, but also in the fact that their team has the ability to interact in a smooth, polished fashion.

As they execute their plan, they run into a number of obstacles that threaten their mission. Among problems they must overcome is an accidental injury that resulted when one member of the team did not follow the plan, a number of planning and technology mishaps, and, when the team discovers that Ocean's ex-wife, Tess, is a large personal motivator for his plan, the team's trust in their leader is jeopardized.

In the end, they cohesively come together as a team and successfully improvise to overcome challenges. Their success is based largely on their collective ability to accomplish the mission, and is a powerful, albeit fictional example of what teams can achieve when they are motivated to work together to attain a common goal.

Language of Leadership

- **Facilitator**—One who works to make something easier or less difficult or that assists in promoting the progress of an individual, team, or endeavor
- **Inhibitor**—One that restrains, hinders, suppresses, prohibits, or forbids the expression or actions of others

Considerations in Conflict Resolution

- Make good relationships a first priority.
- Separate people and problems.
- Pay attention to the interests being presented.
- Listen first, talk second.
- Stick to the facts.
- Explore options collaboratively.

Source: Adapted from *Conflict Resolution: Resolving Conflict Rationally and Effectively* (Manktelow, 2008).

"All great relationships, the ones that last over time, require productive conflict in order to grow."

–Patrick Lencioni, author of *The Five Dysfunctions of a Team*

he or she has developed through words and deeds compared to those of the person on the opposite side of the facilitator-inhibitor interface.

Conflict Management and Resolution in the Team Environment

When we think of conflict, we almost always imagine the negative implications of it. But, when handled properly, conflict can have constructive results as well. According to Gary Ludwig, deputy chief of the Memphis (Tennessee) Fire Department and a retired chief paramedic with the city of St. Louis, "[t]he challenge for EMS managers when conflict occurs is not to avoid it, but to look for the opportunities that come along with conflict. Understanding this fact and resolving conflict effectively will result in personal and professional growth as well as greater team cohesion."

Although there are upsides to conflict, it is important to realize that "conflicting goals can quickly turn into personal dislike" (Manktelow, 2008). Additionally, there may be times when a conceptual or perceived conflict occurs between people or groups as a result of ideas and arguments that may be incongruent with what people already know or believe. These misunderstandings contribute to conflict and can be damaging to a team environment. It is often the responsibility of the EMS leader to gather information and facilitate understanding of other points of view between those involved in the conflict that will result in a relatively positive outcome for everyone.

A number of approaches can be taken to resolve conflict. In the 1970s, for example, Kenneth W. Thomas and Ralph H. Kilmann wrote the *Thomas-Kilmann Conflict Mode Instrument*, which identified the primary ways in which people deal with conflict:

- The **competitive**, in which a firm stand is taken
- A more **collaborative** approach, where attempts are made to meet the needs of everyone involved
- Those who take a more **compromising** approach, in which they seek to partially satisfy everyone
- An approach that **accommodates** the needs of others at the expense of the accommodator
- Those who endeavor to **avoid** conflict all together

Each has strengths and weaknesses, and no one of them can be used in every situation. Therefore, it is essential to know that there are many ways to approach a situation. Next, based on the circumstances and people involved, selecting the best approach will enable the EMS provider to attain the best results.

Effective Team Characteristics

- Inspired leadership
- Specific and quantifiable goals
- Commitment and loyalty
- Effective communication
- Open-minded and progressive thinking
- Recognition

Source: Second Class Petty Officer Leadership Course Student Guide (Chief of Naval Education and Training, 1996).

You Are the EMS Leader

You are an EMS leader in an organization that has union ALS and BLS providers. It has come to your attention that a union representative has sent an e-mail to all union members at your organization regarding his representation at disciplinary meetings and hearings for a large number of your providers. In the e-mail, the union representative makes statements that essentially advise the providers that no matter what, their management will blame the line staff for their mistakes, and the line staff will be subsequently punished. The representative basically suggests that management believes that union members are always wrong and will not stand behind them.

1. Although the e-mail was not addressed to you or any other members of the organization's management team, what, if any, action can or would you consider?

2. Do you believe the e-mail to be harmful to the organization or its individual members?

3. Despite the negative undertones, a portion of the e-mail addresses personnel safety, liability, and patient care issues. Does this fact mitigate your feelings concerning the negative statements? Why or why not?

4. Do you believe the union representative was seeking to facilitate personnel safety, liability, and patient care issues or to inhibit cohesion of the organization by driving a wedge between management and labor? Support your answer.

> **"**For long term mutual interest to be recognized and valued, individuals have to perceive their interdependence and be invested in each other's well being.**"**
>
> –Roger T. Johnson and David W. Johnson, 2008, Codirectors, Cooperative Learning Center, University of Minnesota

The X-Team Concept

EMS is in a state of flux. In 2002, Deborah Ancona, Henrik Bresman, and Katrin Kaeufer wrote "The Comparative Advantage of X-Teams" for the *MIT Sloan Management Review*. They discuss the "demands of a new brand of team—one that emphasizes outreach to stakeholders and adapts easily to flatter organizational structures, changing information and increasing complexity," and how such teams can and have served organizations well. Given the emphasis on the EMS Agenda for the Future and the changing scope of practice in contrast to typical inwardly focused teams, the X-team is more externally oriented and adaptive to its surroundings and is perhaps therefore well suited for EMS organizations. A true X-team has external activity, extensive ties, expandable structures, and a flexible membership in which "core members frequently work beside other members of equal or higher rank, and serve on other X-teams as operational members" (Ancona et al., 2002). In the X-team environment, "even when team members are frustrated that a component they have worked on has been dropped, they appreciate knowing about the change and why it has been made" (Ancona et al., 2002).

The power in this type of approach is that "X-team components form a self-reinforcing system" (Ancona et al., 2002) that build both trust and skill among their members. Members aspire to progress to higher rank and greater responsibility and are encouraged by core members to do just that. The reality is that "there are few behaviors that build confidence as well as a personalized expression of belief in an individual" (LaFasto & Larson, 2001). An EMS organization with a desire to groom leaders and allow them to pass from the outer fringes to the core is an X-team of sorts even if they don't realize there is a term for what they are doing. Going forward, as you think about your organization and whether it is currently an X-team in whole or in part, or whether you believe this concept would help you in your efforts to improve your organization, consider this: By trusting our members with important and meaningful responsibility when we select them for projects and elect or appoint them to serve as our leaders, we are building trust and perpetuating the X-team concept at the same time.

Comparing Traditional and X-Teams

Traditional Team	X-Team
Internally focused on trust, cohesion, and efficient work practices	Combination of internal and external activity
Efforts are increased to build close ties among members and create a strong identity	Internal ties are supplemented with both strong and weak ties outside the team
One structural tier with the team versus the environment	Consists of three expandable tiers—the core, operational, and outer-net tiers
Stable membership consisting of leaders and members	Membership is more flexible with movement across the tiers and both in and out of the team
The mechanism for execution is based on coordination among individuals	The mechanism for execution consists of coordination among tiers

Source: Adapted from "The Comparative Advantage of X-Teams" (Ancona et al., 2002).

Wrap-Up

Chapter Summary

In this chapter, we tied much of the rest of the book together as we looked at team building, trust, communication, and conflict resolution. In these areas, the lessons from previous chapters about communication, interpersonal skills, and psychology all come into play. We also looked at the positive and negative power of conflict and the inevitability that conflict will exist in every organization. Finally, we looked at a comparison of the traditional team with a more contemporary X-team approach to illustrate that the team mentality is changing; whether your organizations and the teams within them are more traditional, more contemporary, or some form of hybrid will depend, in great measure, on their makeup, leadership, and the relationship between the leaders and followers.

Why Their Views Matter: About the Authors Cited in the Chapter

Deborah Ancona is the Seley Distinguished Professor in Management at the MIT Sloan School of Management.

Henrik Bresman is a doctoral candidate at the MIT Sloan School of Management and coauthor of "The Comparative Advantage of X-Teams."

Vic Carucci is the national editor of NFL.com. In addition to coauthoring *No Excuses* with Charlie Weiss, he is the coauthor of *Do You Love Football?* with John Gruden and *Sunday Morning Quarterback* with Phil Simms.

Harriet Diamond is coauthor of *Phrases for Motivating and Rewarding Employees* and *Teambuilding That Gets Results*.

Linda Eve Diamond has worked in corporate training for more than 15 years and is the author and coauthor of a number of books, including *Perfect Phrases for Motivating and Rewarding Employees, Rule #1: Stop Talking: A Guide to Listening*, and *Teambuilding That Gets Results*.

Herman Edwards is head coach of the Kansas City Chiefs and former head coach of the New York Jets. He was a driving force behind a number of community programs over the years, including the Herman Edwards Football Camp for underprivileged children. He is the coauthor of *You Play to Win the Game: Leadership Lessons for Success On and Off the Field*.

Roger T. Johnson is a professor in the Department of Curriculum and Instruction at the University of Minnesota. He holds an MA degree from Ball State University and an EdD degree from the University of California at Berkeley. He is codirector of the Cooperative Learning Center.

David W. Johnson is a professor of educational psychology at the University of Minnesota, where he holds the Emma M. Birkmaier Professorship in Educational Leadership. He is codirector of the Cooperative Learning Center. He received an MS degree and a doctorate from Columbia University. He is a past editor of the *American Educational Research Journal*. He has published more than 350 research articles and book chapters and is the author of more than 40 books.

Katrin Kaeufer is a visiting scholar at MIT Sloan School of Management and coauthor of "The Comparative Advantage of X-Teams."

Ralph H. Kilmann is an independent author and consultant. He has been a visiting scholar at the College of Business Administration, California State University at Long Beach. Formerly, he was the George H. Love Professor of Organization and Management at the Joseph M. Katz Graduate School of Business, University of Pittsburgh. He holds BS and MS degrees in industrial administration from Carnegie-Mellon University and a PhD in management from the University of California at Los Angeles.

Frank LaFasto is Senior Vice President of Organization Effectiveness for Cardinal Health, Inc. He has more than 25 years of experience working to improve organizations through the development and sustaining of teams. He is the coauthor of *Teamwork* and *When Teams Work Best: 6000 Team Members and Leaders Tell What It Takes to Succeed*.

Carl Larson is a professor of human communication and is past dean of social sciences at the University of Denver. He was the recipient of the Driscoll Master Educator Award given by the students of the University of Denver. He is the coauthor of *Communication and Negotiation, Collaborative Leadership: How Citizens and Civic Leaders Can Make a Difference*, and *When Teams Work Best: 6000 Team Members and Leaders Tell What It Takes to Succeed*.

Patrick Lencioni is the author of a number of best-selling books, including *The Five Dysfunctions of a Team*. In addition to his work as an author, he consults and speaks to thousands of people each year on topics relating to leadership, teamwork, management, and organization development. He has served on the National Board of Directors for the Make-A-Wish Foundation of America. He is president of The Table Group of San Francisco.

Abraham Lincoln was the 16th president of the United States. He was assassinated while in office on April 15, 1865. Before becoming president, he was a captain in the Illinois Militia and an Illinois State Representative as well as a U.S. Representative. Lincoln knew the value of surrounding himself with the best and the brightest in his cabinet and prevailed on them often for advice. Lincoln is perhaps best known for his role in ending slavery and his eloquent addresses that have long been remembered and referred to.

Vince Lombardi, Jr. is the son of the legendary football coach Vince Lombardi, whose uncanny ability to motivate others, along with his insatiable drive for victory, made him the standard against which leaders in every field are measured. He has built a successful career in his own right in law, politics, sports, motivational speaking, and writing. He maintained a law practice while serving in the Minnesota legislature and has held executive positions with the Seattle Seahawks, the NFL Management Council, and the U.S. Football League. He is the author of *The Lombardi Rules, What It Takes to Be #1*, and *The Essential Vince Lombardi*.

Gary Ludwig is deputy fire chief of the Memphis (Tennessee) Fire Department. He has more than 30 years of experience in fire and EMS, including 25 years with the city of St. Louis, from which he retired at the rank of chief paramedic. He served as president of the IAFC EMS Section. He regularly writes on the topic of leadership for national trade magazines and shares his insights at conferences throughout the United States.

James Manktelow is the founder and CEO of Mind Tools, an organization whose mission is to help people around the world learn the practical skills needed to excel in their careers. Since its inception, Mind Tools has become a popular and frequently visited career skills website.

Kenneth W. Thomas is coauthor of *The Thomas-Kilmann Conflict Mode Instrument*, which provides an understanding of how different conflict-handling modes, or styles, affect interpersonal and group dynamics and for learning how to select the most appropriate style for a given situation.

Charlie Weiss is the head football coach at Notre Dame University. He previously served as an assistant on the New York Giants and Jets coaching staffs under Bill Parcells and as offensive coordinator for the New England Patriots, who won three Super Bowls in four years. Charlie Weiss is coauthor of the book *No Excuses*.

Chapter 11

Preparing for the Future of EMS

"There are no such things as limits to growth, because there are no limits on the human capacity for intelligence, imagination, and wonder.**"**

—Ronald Reagan

Introduction

As we move forward into the future of EMS, we have the benefit of the last few decades of experience and the lessons we have learned through the successes and shortfalls of modern EMS. We have the foundation built by past leaders, and now, we too must construct the framework for the EMS of the future. My own journey in EMS began at a training center where I took an enhanced advanced first aid and emergency course. This training center was the creation of a few local EMS providers who had a passion for EMS and for teaching. It was held after hours in a high school, and our primary lectures were presented in a lobby common area. We used the hallways and some classrooms for our practical training. Each night, half the students were assigned to come in early to carry the equipment down from a storage cage and set it up, while the other half were assigned to pack it all up and carry it back upstairs to be locked away until our next class. Over the years, much of the equipment was donated and the staff of volunteer instructors grew. Today, the humble beginnings of that training center have greatly expanded. The center now has its own building and a full-time staff that teaches basic and continuing education programs to thousands of students each year. Had it not been for the vision, passion, and leadership of the instructors, EMS training and competency in my county would not be what it is today. I am certain that the success of these great EMS leaders, while inspiring, is not completely unique. If you ask EMS providers around the country about their training in the 1970s and 1980s, you likely will hear similar stories of creativity, imagination, and determination to serve the cause of EMS.

EMS Agenda for the Future—Areas for Ongoing Development

- Integration of health services
- EMS research
- Legislation and regulation
- System finance
- Human resources
- Medical direction
- Education systems
- Prevention
- Public access
- Communications systems
- Evaluation

The Agenda for the Future

In 1996, a group of EMS leaders from around the country collaborated and developed the EMS Agenda for the Future. They took the lessons of the past and their combined experience and vision and used them as the basis for their work. They created an outline of 14 areas of EMS and looked at where we have been, where we are, and where they envision EMS going into the future.

It is clear from the list that leaders in virtually every aspect of EMS can and must play a role in taking the lessons of the past and combining them with the resources of the present to facilitate the vision for the future. As a followup, the National Highway Traffic Safety Administration has developed an implementation guide and a number of other related resources that EMS leaders can and should become familiar with and use in guiding their organizations into the future of EMS.

The National EMS Scope of Practice Model

The National EMS Scope of Practice Model was developed by a group of EMS professionals and others from around the country to define the scope of practice for each nationally recognized EMS

Leadership Through the Hollywood Lens

The movie *Back to the Future* is a mix of comedy, action, and science fiction. Its main character, Marty McFly (played by Michael J. Fox), a high school student, befriends an eccentric scientist, Dr. Emmet Brown (Christopher Lloyd), who has spent his life developing a time machine. When Doc Brown finally tests his experiment in the wee hours of the morning, he is attacked by the people from whom he stole plutonium to make the time machine work. Eventually, Marty winds up in the time machine and travels from the 1980s back to 1955. Through a number of encounters with his parents, who are teenagers in 1955, he disrupts the time-space continuum. First, with potentially devastating consequences, McFly accidentally prevents his parents from meeting for the first time. However, they ultimately do meet, but under different circumstances and the course of history is changed forever.

Fast-forward to Marty's return to the 1980s: despite his changes to history, McFly's family is still together, and his parents are actually happier than they were prior to Marty's time travels. His father, George McFly (Crispin Glover), wrote science fiction stories as a child, and before Marty's time travels, he was afraid to let anyone read them. Thus, they were never published. When Marty returns to the present, his father has transformed into a successful and published writer. Although this film is only fiction, there is a practical message that can be applied to the real world—that one's actions can and do have an effect on the future. The actions and decisions of past EMS leaders paved the road to the present, and we, as the EMS leaders of today, will need to make decisions and take actions that will affect the course of the future history of EMS.

licensure level. In addition to the task force of experts from around the country, the technical advisory group, and the administrative and national review teams, there was broad input from community testimony. Among other things, the model supports the EMS Agenda for the Future by providing a continuation of the commitment to its implementation. It also supports four levels of EMS provider and a system of licensure for EMS personnel commonly found in other allied health professions.

Among the reasons for the creation of the National Scope of Practice Model was that the research in putting it together revealed 39 different licensure levels among EMTs and paramedics across as many states. This variety has been found to contribute to public confusion, reciprocity difficulties, increased challenges to professional mobility, and decreased efficiency at times caused by duplication of effort.

As with any change in any field, there are a variety of views of the model's positives and negatives. In my view, something of this significance should have occasional widespread but respectful discourse to facilitate a more comprehensive end result. For example, through the consensus-building process, the proposal of an advanced practice paramedic has been tabled until evidence-based research can be done to validate the need for this skill level. According to William E. Brown, Jr. (2008), who is the executive director of the National Registry of Emergency Medical Technicians, "a thorough understanding of the Scope of Practice (SOP) Model and its benefits are critical to successfully making the transition, so EMS professionals and other stakeholders should familiarize themselves with these documents." Whether you agree or disagree in whole or in part with the National EMS Scope of Practice Model as it was drafted or amended, as an EMS leader it is important not only to embrace the process thus far but to participate in it going forward. The vision of those who started the process as well as the input and feedback of EMS professionals from across the nation has served to modify and improve the model for the greater good.

National EMS Scope of Practice Levels of Licensure

- Emergency Medical Responder (EMR)
- Emergency Medical Technician (EMT)
- Advanced Emergency Medical Technician (AEMT)
- Paramedic

Source: The National EMS Scope of Practice Model (2007).

Language of Leadership

- **Licensure**—The act of a state granting an entity permission to do something that the entity could not legally do without such permission. Licensing is generally viewed by legislative bodies as a regulatory effort to protect the public from potential harm. In the health care delivery system, an individual who is licensed tends to enjoy a certain amount of autonomy in delivering health care services. Conversely, the licensed individual must satisfy ongoing requirements that ensure certain minimum levels of expertise. A license is generally considered a privilege, not a right.

- **Regulation**—Either a rule or a statute that prescribes the management, governance, or operating parameters for a given group; tends to be a function of administrative agencies to which a legislative body has delegated authority to promulgate rules and regulations to "regulate a given industry or profession." Most regulations are intended to protect the public health, safety, and welfare.

- **Scope of practice**—Defined parameters of various duties or services that may be provided by an individual with specific credentials. Whether regulated by rule, statute, or court decision, it represents the limits of services an individual may legally perform.

Source: The National EMS Scope of Practice Model (2007).

Suggested Reading from the National Highway Traffic Safety Administration

- Emergency Medical Services (EMS) Agenda for the Future
- Implementation Guide for the EMS Agenda for the Future
- Education Agenda for the Future: A Systems Approach
- Trauma System Agenda for the Future
- National Research Agenda
- Guide for Preparing Medical Directors
- Emergency Medical Services Outcomes Evaluation

Leadership Lessons from History

In Ireland in the 1960s, Dr. J. Frank Pantridge was a driving force behind a prehospital care program designed to increase heart attack survival through prehospital intervention. Over the next decade or so, a number of doctors across the United States began developing variations on the theme. Their work was perhaps the beginnings of the modern era of EMS. Although the first fire department–based paramedics were said to be in Florida under the direction of Dr. Eugene Nagel, perhaps the most widely known program, due in large part to the television series *Emergency*, was in Los Angeles. Whether in Belfast, Miami, Los Angeles, or any of the other areas of the country or the world where this concept was being tried, it was the bold leadership of the doctors and public officials who made it happen. In Los Angeles, for example, a lot of time and effort on the part of the fire department, hospitals, and lawmakers went into the program. But it was not until the signing of the Wedworth-Townsend Act by then Governor Ronald Reagan that the California program truly began.

By examining our organization's history, it is clear that leadership is not a foreign concept to EMS; in fact, it has been central to our existence from the beginning of EMS's modern age. In the early days, the concept of an individual, other than a doctor or nurse, providing medical care sparked a significant debate about a number of areas related to, among other things, scope of practice. Clearly the changes proposed at the time were hot-button issues that generated strong opinions. However, when the debate was concluded, a consensus was reached and legislation, policies, and procedures were enacted. As leaders in EMS today, we have the benefit of the trials and errors of our modern EMS forebearers to consider together with our own views, experiences, passions, and visions for the future of EMS in this country. Just as we are discussing the names and visions of people who affected EMS today, so too will the leaders of tomorrow be discussing the impact that today's leaders in EMS will have on them.

Working Together Today for a Better Tomorrow

For EMS leaders of today, the importance of working together cannot be overemphasized. However, this concept is as challenging as it is important because we have representatives of a variety of generations active in the profession, each of whom has a different perspective and different needs, desires, and approaches to the common challenges that we face together. There are representatives of the Silent Generation, the Baby Boomers, Generation X, and the Millennial Generation (Generation Y) throughout EMS on the local, state, and national levels.

In contemporary EMS, as in society, generational awareness is a key to successful leadership. Without an understanding of other generations, there will be a higher likelihood of rifts between coworkers and leaders alike. For example, some generational clashes are as simple as a miscommunication of tone or style, whereas others might be the result of questioning one another's motives or even being closed to an opinion different from one's own. Rifts, whether generational, personal, or otherwise, can and will happen despite our best efforts to prevent them. However, by keeping an open mind and being flexible in your role as an EMS leader, you can both minimize their occurrence and be better prepared to handle them when they arise.

Defining the Generations

- **Silent Generation—** Born between approximately 1930 and 1945, these "elders" of EMS are known for their commitment, responsibility, and conformity.
- **Baby Boomers—**Born between approximately 1946 and 1963, these members of the EMS community tend to be perfectionists and have strong personal values. They tend to embrace a team-based approach.
- **Generation X—**Born between approximately 1964 and 1979, this generation has a generally skeptical attitude toward authority, and individuals are cautious in their commitments. They lean more toward "free agency" than they do company or organizational loyalty. They tend to be ambitious and independent.
- **Millennial Generation—** Born between 1980 and the present, they are sometimes called Generation Y or the Eco-Boom Generation. They tend to be drawn to organizations that put purpose above profit. They are technologically savvy and want to make a difference.

Source: Adapted from *Defining a Generation: Tips for Uniting our Multi-Generational Workforce*.

"*Choose your leadership actions based on what people need, not what you're most comfortable with.***"**

–Leslie Jaffee and Karl Krumm, authors of *Leadership Post 9/11*

You Are the EMS Leader

One of your younger providers shows a lot of promise. Her skills are excellent, and her instructors and partners alike give her high marks for knowledge level. Unfortunately, there are many who also say that as good as she is, she has a lot to learn about dealing with others and following organizational policies and procedures when she feels they don't make sense, are a waste of time, or are just plain silly. To complicate matters, when more experienced people have attempted to correct mistakes and provide guidance about why certain things are done certain ways, she shrugs off the support with an "I know" response that doesn't ring true. She is placed with good partners in the hope that not only will she learn from them, but that the more seasoned partners will provide a safety net for her "know-it-all" attitude until maturity kicks in.

The situation comes to a head when, despite policy, she fails to verify an address to which her team is dispatched. While responding, her partner attempts to tell her that the address where they are going is incorrect. She ignores the partner and insists on responding to the unverified address. Her error causes a delayed response to the patient. Fortunately, the patient's situation was not life threatening and he did not suffer complications as a result of the delayed response.

Her partner attempts to use the situation as a learning opportunity but, as usual, she does not respond well. The partner has had enough and comes to you for guidance and perhaps intervention.

1. *What is your initial reaction, and what are your thoughts on the situation?*

2. *What guidance do you provide the partner?*

3. *Describe how not only experience level but also generational differences would affect your approach to this situation.*

4. *What actions do you take as the EMS leader, and how do you factor the violation of policy into the equation?*

5. *Would your actions change if the patient's condition were affected by the delay caused by the provider's behavior? Why or why not?*

Wrap-Up

Chapter Summary

Throughout history, there are successes and failures, each of which provides valuable opportunities for learning and growth. From the first civilian ambulance services of the 1860s in Cincinnati and New York City, to the Highway Safety Act of 1966 that established the foundation for the modern era of EMS in America, to the National Scope of Practice Model that has set the stage for the future, the best and brightest of EMS's past and present have come together to change with the times and create a vision for the future. Although generational rifts have occurred and invariably will continue to occur, these should be embraced as a means of creating energy to drive spirited discourse that will result in the necessary consensus between the experience of the past and the leaders and providers of the future. To best facilitate success, EMS leaders must understand the impact of the past and present on the future as well as how to best lead and motivate the multigenerational EMS workforce.

Why Their Views Matter: About the Authors Cited in the Chapter

William E. Brown, Jr. is the executive director of NREMT. He is a former U.S. Air Force pararescue man who served one tour in Viet Nam and was decorated for heroism for a rescue behind enemy lines. He previously served as the paramedic program director at Youngtown State University in Ohio and has experience as an emergency room nurse and as a paramedic. He has published a number of articles in a variety of magazines and been published in peer review journals.

Leslie S. Jaffee has more than two decades of experience as a consultant and writer on a number of business and nonprofit environments. Her focus is on enabling transformation and achievement of results. Included in her broad experience is coaching and leadership development with Jewish Funds for Justice and the Los Angeles Alliance for a New Economy.

Karl J. Krumm has more than 20 years of experience consulting with individuals, teams, and organizations on topics that include managing a diverse workforce in today's rapidly changing world, executive selection, management training, and organizational design. He is currently a senior associate with Claire Raines Associates.

Eugene Nagel was perhaps best known for his influence in establishing the first mobile intensive care unit in Miami that would allow voice-based telemetry to provide oversight to field units in areas like emergency coronary care. He was one of the original editorial advisory board members for *EMS Magazine* and served the University of Miami and the Miami Fire Department with distinction.

James Francis "Frank" Pantridge was a physician and cardiologist from Ireland who played a key role in prehospital emergency care and the invention of the defibrillator. He was both educated and served as a professor at Queen's University of Belfast. In 1957, he and Dr. John Geddes introduced the modern system of cardiopulmonary resuscitation. He was known in many circles as the "father of emergency medicine."

Ronald Reagan was the 40th president of the United States. He served as a captain in the U.S. Army and was governor of California before being elected to the presidency in 1980. Reagan used his experience as an actor to hone his communications skills. He was known as the Great Communicator for his ability to present his ideas in an understandable way that was often illustrated with a joke or a story.

Glossary

Burnout—Occurs when coping mechanisms no longer buffer job stressors, which can compromise personal health and well being

Co-acting Team—A team, such as in bowling or wrestling, in which members work independently for an overall common purpose

Cohesiveness—The act or state of sticking together tightly

Collaboration—To work jointly with others

Consensus—Group solidarity in sentiment or belief

Earned Authority—Authority that grows out of the respect, credibility, and leadership qualities that encourage others to follow

Empathy—Projection of one's own personality into the personality of another to understand him or her better; ability to share in another's emotions or feelings

Ethical Behavior—Behavior judged as good, right, just, honorable, and praiseworthy

Ethics—A system or set of moral principles

Ethos—The distinguishing character, sentiment, moral nature, or guiding beliefs of a person, group, or institution

Etiquette—The forms, manners, and ceremonies established by convention as acceptable or required in social relations, in a profession, or in official life

Facilitator—One who works to make something easier or less difficult or who assists in promoting the progress of an individual, team, or endeavor

Field Training Officer (FTO)—An experienced or senior member of an organization who is responsible for the training of a junior or probationary-level member

General Impression—Impression of the patient's condition that is formed when first approaching the patient; based on the patient's environment, chief complaint, and appearance

Indicator—An objective behavior or outcome that can be measured to determine compliance with a standard

Inhibitor—One that restrains, hinders, suppresses, prohibits, or forbids the expressions or actions of others

Integrity—Uncompromising adherence to moral and ethical principles; soundness of moral character; honesty

Interacting Team—A team, such as in basketball or soccer, in which members have interdependent roles

Intimate Space—Generally up to 18 inches and reserved for interactions with family and close friends

Legal Authority—The official authority that is inherent to the position or office that the leader holds

Licensure—The act of a state granting an entity permission to do something that the entity could not legally do without such permission. Licensing is generally viewed by legislative bodies as a regulatory effort to protect the public from potential harm. In the healthcare delivery system, an individual who is licensed tends to enjoy a certain amount of autonomy in delivering healthcare services. Conversely, the licensed individual must satisfy ongoing requirements that ensure certain minimum levels of expertise. A license is generally considered a privilege and not a right.

Logos—Speech, word, reason. In ancient Greek philosophy, reason is the controlling principle in the universe.

Management—The act or art of conducting, handling, controlling, or directing something through the judicious use of means to accomplish an end

Mentor—A trusted counselor or guide

Moral Authority—Derived from the leader's sense of responsibility to do what is proper and to step forward and take the lead even when not required

Morals—Pertaining to or concerned with the principles of right conduct or the distinction between right and wrong

Pathos—An element in experience or in artistic representation evoking pity or compassion; an emotion of sympathetic pity

Perception—Mental grasp of objects and qualities by means of the senses

Personal Space—Where most interpersonal interactions take place; generally ranges from approximately 18 inches to about 4 feet

Preceptor—A teacher or tutor

Protégé—A person guided and helped, especially in the furtherance of his or her career, by another, more influential person

Public Space—The area in which things like large audience interactions take place; generally more than 12 feet

Regulation—Either a rule or a statute that prescribes the management, governance, or operating parameters for a given group; tends to be a function of administrative agencies to which a legislative body has delegated authority to promulgate rules and regulations to "regulate a given industry or profession." Most regulations are intended to protect the public health, safety, and welfare

Scope of Practice—Defined parameters of various duties or services that may be provided by an individual with specific credentials. Whether regulated by rule, statute, or court decision, it represents the limits of services an individual may legally perform

Social Space—Area in which more formal interactions take place; ranges from 4 to 12 feet

Standard—A generalized goal that is an achievable model of excellence and is used to define expectations

Stress—Any event or situation that places extraordinary demands on a person's mental or emotional resources

Stressor—An emotional stimulus that affects an organism in ways that are physically or psychologically injurious, usually producing anxiety, tension, or psychological arousal

Supervision—The action or process of watching, directing, or guiding workers or the work done by others

Team—A small task group in which members have a common purpose, interdependent roles, and complementary skills

Threshold—An established level or percentage of acceptable compliance that indicates when further evaluation should be initiated

Trainee—One that is being trained, especially for a job

Trend—A prevailing tendency

Trust—A firm belief or confidence in the honesty, integrity, reliability, or justice of another person or thing

Unethical Behavior—Behavior judged to be wrong, unjust, dishonorable, or failing to meet an obligation

Values—The abstract concepts of what is right, worthwhile, or desirable; principles or standards; social principles, goals, or standards held or accepted by an individual, class, or society

Vision—The ability to perceive something not actually visible, as through mental acuteness or keen foresight

References & Resources

Adubato, S. (2006). *Make the connection: Improve your communication at home and at work.* New York, NY: Barnes & Noble.

Alder, M., & Fratus, M. (2007, June). The impact of department culture on fireground safety. *Fire Engineering,* 83–91.

Alexander, M. (2006). *Foundations for the practice of EMS education.* Upper Saddle River, NJ: Pearson Prentice Hall.

American Psychological Association. (2004). Obeying and resisting malevolent orders. Retrieved September 3, 2008, from: http://www.psychologymatters.org/milgram.html

Ancona, D., Bresman, H., & Kaeufer, K. (2007, Spring). The comparative advantage of X-teams. *MIT Sloan Management Review, 43,* 33–39.

Ardolino, E. (Director). (1992). *Sister act* [Motion Picture]. United States: Touchstone Pictures.

Balderama, A. (2008). Burned out on the job. Retrieved May 19, 2008, from: http://www.jobs.aol.com

Barishansky, R. M. (2006, November). Paying it forward: The importance of being a mentor. *EMS Magazine,* 79.

Becknell, J. (2008, March). True quality comes from within. *Best Practices in Emergency Services,* 11–13, 26.

Bellisario, D. P. (Producer). (2007). Blind side [Television series episode]. In *JAG.* Hollywood, CA: CBS Studios.

Biebee, D. (2002, January). How to increase phone sales. Retrieved May 28, 2008, from: http://www.lctmag.com/index.cfm?action=article&type=view&sid=0&aid=b0ce258c-26fb-46f1-bf47-a65be54a1799

Blanchard, K. (1985). *Leadership and the one minute manager.* New York: William Morrow and Company.

Blanchard, K. (1999). *Heart of a leader: Insights on the art of influence.* Escondito, CA: Honor Books.

Blass, T. (2002, March–April). The man who shocked the world. *Psychology Today, 35*(2), 68–74.

Bledsoe, B., Porter, R., & Cherry, R. (2003). *Essentials of paramedic care.* Upper Saddle River, NJ: Pearson Education.

Boxman, L., & Rogers, J. (2005, March). The road to greatness. *fireEMS,* 37–39.

Brophy, J. R. (2007, September–October). The behavior allowed becomes the standard. *9-1-1 Magazine,* 32–34.

Brophy, J. R. (2008, April). Quality improvement through education and positive reinforcement. *9-1-1 Magazine,* 30–32.

Brown, W. (2008, September). From fragmentation to unity: How to make the transition to the national EMS scope of practice model. *JEMS,* 46–48.

Browner, B. D., Pollak, A. N., & Gupton, C. L. (Eds.). (2002). *Emergency care and transportation of the sick and injured* (8th ed.). Sudbury, MA: Jones and Bartlett Publishers.

Buckman, III, J. M. (Ed.). (2006). *Chief fire officer's desk reference.* Sudbury, MA: Jones and Bartlett Publishers.

Burdick, M. (2007, August). Tremendous trivials. *Fire Chief,* 60–64.

Bush, G. (1999). *All the best, George Bush: My life in letters and other writings.* New York: Lisa Drew/Scribner.

Cannon, L. (2004, June 6). Why Reagan was the "great communicator." *USA Today.* Retrieved February 1, 2008, from: http://usatoday.com.

Carrison, D., & Walsh, R. (1999). *Business leadership the Marine Corps way.* New York: MJF Books.

Cason, D. (2006). *Foundations of education: An EMS approach.* St. Louis, MO: Mosby JEMS Elsevier.

Champoux, J. E. (2006). *Organizational behavior* (3rd ed.). Mason, OH: Thomson South-Western.

Chapleau, W., Burba, A. C., Pons, P. T., & Page, D. (2008). *The paramedic.* New York: McGraw-Hill.

Chief of Naval Education and Training. (1996). *Second class petty officer leadership course student guide.* Pensacola, FL: Department of the Navy.

Conger, J., Spreitzer, G., & Lawler, E. (Eds.) (1999). *Leader's change handbook*. San Francisco, CA: Jossey-Bass.

Costello, R. B. (1992). *Random House Webster's college dictionary*. New York: Random House.

Crouchman, J. (2005). [EMT-Basic Class Lecture]. Presented at Meadowlands Hospital, Secaucus, NJ.

Curtis, B. (Ed.). (2002). *A call for excellence*. Nashville, TN: Rutledge Hill Press.

Dernocoeur, K. B. (1996). *Streetsense*. Redmond, WA: Laing Research Services.

Diamond, L., & Diamond, H. (2007). *Teambuilding that gets results*. Naperville, IL: Sourcebooks.

Dick, T. (2005). *People care: Career-friendly practices for professional caregivers*. Van Nuys, CA: Cygnus Business Media.

Dick, T. (2005, January). U-turns: What do you do when you're wrong? *EMS Magazine*, 34.

Dourado, P., & Blackburn, P. (2005). *Seven secrets of inspired leaders*. New York: MJF Books.

Dresser, M. (1995). *Essential teachings: His holiness the Dalai Lama*. New York: MJF Books.

Drewry, D. L. (2004). *The chief petty officer's manual* (3rd ed.). Pensacola, FL: Professional Management Spectrum.

Eastham, J. N., & Champion, H. R. (1997). *A leadership guide to quality improvement for emergency medical services systems*. Washington, DC: National Highway Traffic Safety Administration.

Edwards, H., & Smith, S. (2005). *You play to win the game: Leadership lessons for success on and off the field*. New York: McGraw-Hill.

Elgin, S. (1997). *How to disagree without being disagreeable*. New York: MJF Books.

Evans, B. (2005). Move to licensing will change medics' scope. Retrieved September 9, 2008, from: http://firechief.com/ems/firefighting_move_licensing_change/

Evans, B. (2007, August). On the EMS horizon. *Fire Chief*, 98–105.

FEMA. (2007). *FEMA contracting enhancements and improvements post Katrina*. Retrieved May 28, 2008, from: http://www.fema.gov/media/archives/2007/111607b.shtm

Ferris, G., Davidson, S., & Perrewe, P. (2005, November). Developing political skill at work. *Training*, 40–45.

Finzel, H. (2000). *The top ten mistakes leaders make*. Colorado Springs, CO: NexGen.

Forret, M., & de Janasz, S. (2005). Perceptions of an organization's culture for work and family: Do mentors make a difference? *Career Development International*, 478–492.

Fritz, S., Brown, F., Lunde, J., & Banset, E. (2005). *Interpersonal skills for leadership* (2nd ed.). Upper Saddle River, NJ: Pearson Prentice Hall.

Gardner, H. (1995). *Leading minds: An anatomy of leadership*. New York: Basic Books.

Gertzel, J. (2001, October 19). The psychology of leadership. *The Toronto Star*.

Ginn, C. (2006). Boosting employee performance: 10 reasons employees do not perform as expected. Retrieved December 26, 2006, from: http://biz-eye-view.sbc.com

Giuliani, R. W., & Kurson, K. (2002). *Leadership*. New York: Miramax Books.

Golway, T. (2002). *So others might live*. New York: Basic Books.

Graham, G. (2004). Managing the risky business of EMS: Issues for consideration. In *Proceedings from EMS Today Conference and Exposition*. Salt Lake City, UT.

Graham, P. (2008). Stanley Milgram: The perils of obedience. Retrieved September 3, 2008, from: http://www.paulgraham.com/perils.html

Gray, J. (2002). *Mars and Venus in the workplace: A practical guide for improving communication and getting results at work*. New York: HarperCollins Publishers.

Greene, R., & Vernezze, P. (Eds.). (2004). *The Sopranos and philosophy*. Chicago: Open Court.

Guralink, D. (Ed.). (1974). *New world dictionary of the American language* (2nd ed.). Englewood Cliffs, NJ: Prentice-Hall.

Hafter, J., & Frdor, V. (2004). *EMS and the law.* Sudbury, MA: Jones and Bartlett Publishers.

Haid, C. (Director). (2005, September 28). Compulsion [Television series episode]. In *Criminal minds.* Hollywood, CA: Paramount.

Hansen, M., & Batten, J. (1995). *The master motivator: Secrets of inspiring leadership.* New York: Barnes & Noble.

Hathaway, G. (2004). *Leadership secrets from the executive office.* New York: MJF Books.

Henry, M. C., & Stapleton, E. R. (2004). *EMT prehospital care* (3rd ed.). St. Louis, MO: Mosby Jems.

Holman, T. L. (2002). *Leadership rules of engagement.* Kearney, NE: Morris Publishing.

Humes, J. C. (1997). *Nixon's ten commandments of statecraft.* New York: Simon & Schuster.

Jaffee, L., & Krumm, K. (2002). Leadership post 9/11. Retrieved August 30, 2008, from: http://www.generationsatwork.com/articles/leadership.htm

Johnson, C. E. (2005). *Meeting the ethical challenges of leadership.* Thousand Oaks, CA: Sage Publications.

Johnson, D., & Johnson, R. (2008). Conflict resolution. Retrieved June 2, 2008, from: http://www.co-operation.org/pages/conflict.html

Kennedy, C. (Ed.). (2002). *Profiles in courage for our time.* New York: Hyperion.

Kets de Vries, M. (2003). *Leaders, fools and impostors.* Lincoln, NE: iUniverse.

King, D. (2000). Defining a generation: Tips for uniting our multi-generational workforce. Retrieved September 9, 2008, from: http://www.careerfirm.com/generations.htm

Kohn, S. E., & O'Connell, V. D. (2005). *6 habits of highly effective bosses.* Franklin Lakes, NJ: Career Press.

Kotter, J. P. (1996). *Leading change.* Boston, MA: Harvard Business School Press.

La Fasto, F., & Larson, C. (2001). *When teams work best.* Thousand Oaks, CA: Sage Publications.

Landsberger, J. (2008). Conflict resolution. Retrieved June 2, 2008, from: http://www.studygs.net/conflres.htm

Leary, D. (Producer). (2004, September 29). Mom. [Television series episode]. In *Rescue me.* Culver City, CA: Sony Pictures Television.

Lefton, L. A. (1991). *Psychology* (4th ed.). Needham Heights, MA: Allyn and Bacon.

Lencioni, P. (2002). *The five dysfunctions of a team.* San Francisco, CA: Jossey-Bass.

Lichtenberg, R., & Stone, G. (1998). *Work would be great if it weren't for the people.* New York: Barnes & Noble.

Limmer, D., & LeBaudour, J. (2007). *EMT complete: A basic worktext.* Upper Saddle River, NJ: Pearson Education.

Limmer, D., & O'Keefe, M. (2007). *Emergency care* (10th ed.). Upper Saddle River, NJ: Pearson Prentice Hall.

Lombardi, Jr., V. (2005). *The Lombardi rules.* New York: McGraw-Hill.

Lowe, T. (Ed.). (2006). Principles for leading radical change. *Get motivated workbook.* Tampa, FL: Get Motivated Seminars.

Ludwig, G. (2004, November). Count to 10 before you discipline. *JEMS*, 24.

Ludwig, G. (2005, December). Conflict can be a good thing. *JEMS*, 16.

Ludwig, G. (2006, November). [Letter to the Editor]. *JEMS.*

Maggiore, W. A. (2006, March). Hazing, horseplay, & harassment. *EMS Insider*, 2–3.

Magnuson, S. (2007). Crisis management: FEMA chief promises improved disaster response. *National Defense.* Retrieved May 28, 2008, from: http://goliath.ecnext.com/coms2/summary_0199-6979917_ITM

Manktelow, J. (2003). Leadership styles: Using the right one for your situation. Retrieved February 15, 2007, from: http://www.mindtools.com/pages/article/newLDR_84.htm

Manktelow, J. (2008). *Conflict resolution: Resolving conflict rationally and effectively.* Retrieved June 2, 2008, from: http://www.mindtools.com/pages/article/newLDR_81.htm

Marshall, P. (Director). (1994). *Renaissance man* [Motion Picture]. Burbank, CA: Touchstone Pictures.

McCain, J., & Salter, M. (2005). *Character is destiny.* New York: Random House.

McCauley, C., & Van Velsor, E. (Ed.). (2004). *Handbook of leadership development* (3rd ed.). San Francisco, CA: Jossey-Bass.

McDowell, R. (1993). Concepts in EMS quality management. *Quality Management in Prehospital Care,* 14–28.

McManus, P. (2006). Mentor's message: Coaching as a lifelong learning process. In *Coaching people.* Boston, MA: Harvard Business School Press.

McManus, P. (2006). *Coaching people.* Boston, MA: Harvard Business School Press.

Michelli, J. A. (2007). *The Starbucks experience.* New York: McGraw-Hill Books.

Mish, F. C. (Ed.). (1993). *Merriam Webster's collegiate dictionary* (10th ed.). Springfield, MA: Merriam Webster.

National Highway Traffic Safety Administration. (1996). *Emergency medical services agenda for the future.* Washington, DC: United States Department of Transportation.

National Highway Traffic Safety Administration. (2007). *National EMS scope of practice model.* Washington, DC: United States Department of Transportation.

Nelson, D. E. (2008). *Appreciative supervision.* Kansas City, MO.

Nepon, B., & Eberly, B. (2008). *Field training officer: Tips and techniques for FTO's preceptors, and mentors.* Sudbury, MA: Jones and Bartlett Publishers.

New York State Training Council. (2005). *Roles and responsibilities of the mentor and protégé.* Retrieved May 27, 2008, from: http://www.nystc.org/mentor/roles.htm

Pachter, B., & Magee, S. (2000). *The power of positive confrontation.* New York: MJF Books.

Page, J. O. (2002). *The magic of 3 a.m.* Carlsbad, CA: JEMS Communications.

Pfeiffer, W., & Jones, J. (Eds.). (1981). *A handbook of structured experiences for human relations training.* San Diego, CA: University Associates.

Pockell, L., & Avila, A. (Eds.). (2007). *The 100 greatest leadership principles of all time.* New York: Warner Business Books.

Pollak, A., Gulli, B., Chatelain, L., & Stratford, C. (2005). *Emergency care and transportation of the sick and injured* (9th ed.). Sudbury, MA: Jones and Bartlett Publishers.

Quindlen, A. (2007, January). Contrition as leadership. Retrieved January 8, 2009, from: http://www.newsweek.com/id/56700

Quinn, R. E., Faerman, S. R., Thompson, M. P., & McGrath, M. R. (1990). *Becoming a master manager: A competency framework.* New York: John Wiley & Sons.

Reagan, R. (1981, January 20). Inaugural address. Retrieved July 29, 2007, from: http://www.presidency.ucsb.edu

Reicher, S., Platow, M., & Haslam, S. (2007, July 31). The new psychology of leadership. *Scientific American Mind.* Retrieved May 12, 2008, from: www.sciam.com

Reynolds, G., & Gelbart, L. (Producers). (1975). Change of Command [Television series episode]. In *MASH.* Beverly Hills, CA: 20th Century Fox.

Roberts, A. (2003). *Hitler & Churchill: Secrets of leadership.* London: Weidenfeld & Nicolson.

Roberts, W. (2002). *The best advice for leaders.* New York: MJF Books.

Salka, J. (2004). *First in, last out.* New York: Penguin Group.

Schaffer, G. (2006). Mentoring medics. In *Proceedings from EMS expo*. Las Vegas, NV: Cygnus Public Safety Group.

Scott, T. (Director). (1995). *Crimson tide* [Motion Picture]. Burbank, CA: Hollywood Pictures.

Snyder, D. R., & Christmas, C. (Eds.). (2003). *Geriatric education for emergency medical services.* Sudbury, MA: Jones and Bartlett Publishers.

Soder, R. (2001). *The language of leadership.* San Francisco, CA: Jossey-Bass.

Soderbergh, S. (Director). (2000). *Erin Brokovich* [Motion Picture]. Universal City, CA: Universal Studios.

Soderbergh, S. (Director). (2001). *Ocean's 11* [Motion Picture]. United States: Warner Bros. Pictures.

Sonnenfeld, B. (Director). (1997). *Men in black* [Motion Picture]. United States: Columbia Pictures.

Stanko, J. (2000). *So many leaders, so little leadership.* Mobile, AL: Evergreen Press.

Straker, D. (2007). Leadership styles. Retrieved January 12, 2008, from: http://changingminds.org/disciplines/leadership/styles/leadership_styles.htm

Taranto, J., & Leo, L. (Eds.). (2005). *Presidential leadership.* New York: Free Press.

Tribus, M. (1984). Reducing Deming's 14 points to practice (Part II). Retrieved May 24, 2008, from: http://deming.ces.clemson.edu/pub/den/red14points.pdf

Van Wagner, K. (2007). Leadership theories. Retrieved February 16, 2008, from: http://psychology.about.com/od/leadership/p/leadtheories.htm?p=1

Wareing, I., Davies, M., et al. (2007). Mentoring: A discussion paper. Retrieved May 27, 2008, from: http://www.growconnect.com.au/mentor.html

Weisinger, H. (2000). *The power of positive criticism.* New York: MJF Books.

Weiss, C., & Carucci, V. (2006). *No excuses: One man's incredible rise through the NFL to head coach of Notre Dame.* New York: HarperCollins Publishers.

West, S. (Director). (1999). *The general's daughter* [Motion Picture]. United States: Paramount.

Wikipedia. (2008, April 5). Field training officer. Retrieved May 26, 2008, from: http://en.wikipedia.org/wiki/Field_Training_Officer

Wilson, W. (1918, January 8). President Wilson's fourteen points. Retrieved July 29, 2007, from: http://www.lib.byu.edu/~rdh/wwi/1918/14points.html

Wilson, W. (1918, January 8). President Woodrow Wilson's fourteen points. Retrieved August 21, 2008, from: http://www.yale.edu/lawweb/avalon/wilson14.htm

Wolf, D. (2006). *Succession planning: Mentoring and educating younger fire officers for the chief's position.* Retrieved March 1, 2006, from: http://www.firehouse.com

Woolf, H. B. (Ed.). (1974). *The Merriam-Webster dictionary.* New York: Wallaby Books.

Woolfe, L. (2002). *Leadership secrets from the Bible.* New York: MJF Books.

Wren, J. T. (1995). *The leader's companion: Insights on leadership through the ages.* New York: Simon & Schuster.

Yaverbaum, E. (2006). *Leadership secrets of the world's most successful CEOs.* New York: Barnes & Noble.

Yokley, R., & Sutherland, R. (2008). *Emergency! Behind the scene.* Sudbury, MA: Jones and Bartlett Publishers.

Yukl, G. (2006). *Leadership in organizations* (6th ed.). Upper Saddle River, NJ: Pearson Prentice Hall.

Zemeckis, R. (Director). (1985). *Back to the future.* [Motion Picture]. Universal City, CA: Universal Studios.

Zhu, W., May, D., & Avolino, B. (2004). The impact of ethical behavior on employee outcomes: The roles of psychological empowerment and authenticity. *Journal of Leadership and Organizational Studies, 11*(1), 16–26.

Index

Credits